THE ESSENTIAL 11+

VOCABULARY EXPANDER

THEMED VOCABULARY

Book 1

The Essential 11+ Vocabulary Expander Book 1

First published 2021

by Foxton Books
London, UK

ISBN: 978-1-83925-078-1

Author: Jan Webley
Interior designer: Maryke Goldie

www.foxtonbooks.co.uk

Contents

Introduction

This book is an essential tool for vocabulary expansion. Your child's command of vocabulary is at the heart of 11+ success, as many English and Verbal Reasoning questions test children's understanding of word meanings. It has been estimated that up to 60 % of 11+ marks focus on literacy skills, and having a wider vocabulary improves children's ability to understand and access all questions.

Vocabulary is crucial to understanding not only English and Verbal Reasoning papers but also mathematics and other reasoning papers. Together, these tests are used by many local authorities and schools to gauge children's suitability for selective education. The tasks and guidance in this book are designed for Year 4 - 5 children who are working at above expected progress for their age and preparing for 11+ exams. They reflect the type and range of questions children will encounter in both GL and CEM 11+ papers. These tasks are firmly rooted in the English National Curriculum and, in addition, refer to subjects and skills taught in the wider KS2 curriculum, including mathematics, science, history and the arts. Because of this, the book will provide valuable support for preparation for KS2 SATs.

- **Themed Vocabulary**
  Themed vocabulary sections cover all key areas of the curriculum and support the development of complex vocabulary acquisition. Each provides a diverse selection of tasks and challenges which are rooted in the types of questions children can expect to encounter in both GL and CEM 11+ papers.

- **Vocabulary for English and Verbal Reasoning**
  The second half of the book focuses solely on the skills and understanding needed for success in the English and Verbal Reasoning 11+ papers. It covers all key terms and skills children will encounter in the English paper and the vocabulary they will need to access Verbal Reasoning questions. The tasks mirror GL and CEM tasks, including synonyms, antonyms, homographs, prefixes and root words, word relationships, cloze passages, shuffle activities and missing word questions. There is a specific focus on the importance of context to an understanding of vocabulary.

- **Word Games**
  Word games, such as Words within Words, Adding and Taking Letters and Playing with Words, are an excellent way of helping students expand their vocabulary and this selection of games, many of them original, will provide parents with a wealth of ideas which they can use with their children to make preparation for 11+ fun. Many of the games are simple in their design and easy to devise and adapt for everyday use.

- **Answers section**
  Answers are provided, with explanations where appropriate, for all tasks and questions.

GEOGRAPHY AND NATURE

Animals

A Match each of the animals to their **young** by colour coding or drawing a line.

cheetah *cub*	foal *horse*	deer *fawn*	cub *cheetah*
cygnet *swan*	falcon *chick*	goat *goat*	horse *foal*
kid *goat*	fawn *deer*	swan *cygnet*	chick *falcon*

B All animals belong to a **classification**. Identify where these animals belong by adding them to the correct classification list.

~~lizard~~	~~alligator~~	~~wolf~~	~~shark~~	~~salamander~~
~~flamingo~~	~~crow~~	~~owl~~	~~ostrich~~	~~toad~~
~~crocodile~~	~~starling~~	~~snake~~	~~tortoise~~	~~mackerel~~
~~panda~~	~~frog~~	~~newt~~	~~octopus~~	~~whale~~

reptiles	mammals	birds
lizard alligators snake crocodile	wolf panda owl	ostrich crow flamingo starling

fish	amphibians
mackerels salamanders octopush sharks whales	tortoise toad frog newt

C Now complete the following sentences choosing the correct animal classification for each one.

1. _Frog_ start life as eggs and are cold-blooded. They can live on the land or in water.

2. _sharks_ only live in the water and they have fins and scales.

3. Animals who give birth to their young are called _mammals_ and are warm-blooded. They feed their young with milk.

4. The family of _crocodiles_ lay eggs and are cold-blooded. They are often covered in scales or have a horny skin.

5. The category of _crow_ have feathers and wings and most of them can fly.

D Words which sound like their meaning are known as **onomatopoeia**, such as 'crash' or 'bang'. The words we use to describe many animal noises also sound like their meaning. Match the sounds with the animals by drawing lines or colour coding.

snort 2	bat
growl 5	antelope
screech 1	crow
bleat 6	goose
caw 3	bear
honk 4	goat

E Many animal **plurals** are regular and you just add 's'. However, some are irregular and follow different rules. How do you write these animal names as plurals? Identify the rule you are using to make the plural. Think of other words you know that follow that rule.

1. *flamingo* becomes flamingoes

    Rule: add es.

2. *wolf* becomes wolves

    Rule: add ves instead or fes

3. *hippopotamus* becomes hippo pottomi

    Rule: mus become mi

4. All of these words follow the same plural rule. What is it?

    deer   sheep   shrimp   fish   moose

    Rule: do not add anything.

These are completely irregular and do not follow any rule. Can you write out the plural?

5. *ox* becomes   oxen

6. *mouse* becomes   mice

7. *goose* becomes   geese

8. *louse* becomes   lice

F When you have a group of animals, you can use a **collective noun** for them. As with people, there are particular words for different groups of animals. Match up the animals and the collective noun for them by drawing lines or colour coding.

pride 3	wolves 6
army 6	cows 5
pod 4	lions 7
train 5	dolphins 3
herd 2	camels 4
pack 1	ants 2

Trees, Plants and Flowers

A Match all the plants to something you will find **growing** on them. Link them by lines or colour coding.

1 holly bush *3*	*6* acorn
2 cherry tree *4*	*5* conker
3 palm tree *5*	*1* needle
4 oak tree *6*	*2* berry
5 horse chestnut tree *2*	*3* coconut
6 pine tree *1*	*4* blossom

B Look at these trees, plants and flowers and select the right ones to answer the questions below about their **qualities**.

cactus	toadstool	oak	lemon
carnation	bamboo	holly	mistletoe
mushroom	tangerine	daffodil	elm

1. Which two are prickly? _holly_ and _cactus_

2. Which two are citrus? _lemon_ and _tangerine_

3. Which two are fungi? _mushroom_ and _toadstool_

4. Which two are flowers? _carnation_ and _daffodil_

5. Which two are trees? _elm_ and _oak_

6. Which one is a grass? _bamboo_

7. Which one is associated with kissing? _mistletoe_

C Complete the following **cloze passage** by writing in the correct words. Each one can only be used once, so cross them out or highlight them to eliminate them after you have used them. This will help you find the other words more easily.

roots	sprout	climates	water	ingredients
pollinate	sunlight	stem	leaves	cycle

Plants can grow in all kinds of weather and **1.** _climates is_ . The essential

2. _ingredients_ are **3.** _sunlight_ and **4.** _water_ .

When it is planted in the earth, a seed will start to grow **5.** _roots_ which soak up

the water. When the seed is germinated, it will start to **6.** _sprout_ above ground.

The plant is held upright by the **7.** _stem_ and from this **8.** _leaves_

will grow. Insects like bees and butterflies help to **9.** _pollinate_ the plant to start

the life **10.** _cycle_ again.

D Some of these plant and tree words are **homographs**. This means they have more than one meaning. In many cases, the word can belong in 2 different word classes, so it could be both a verb and a noun. Identify the 3 words below which are homographs and write out the 2 different definitions for them.

nectar	palm	jungle	branch
thorn	reed	pine	clover

1. **First homograph:** _palm_

   Meaning 1: _palm of your hand_

   Meaning 2: _palm tree_

2. **Second homograph:** _reed_

   Meaning 1: _reed is a plant_

   Meaning 2: _read 'to read'_

3. **Third homograph:** _branch_

   Meaning 1: _tree's branches_

   Meaning 2: _part of the body_

E Choose the word which is closest in meaning to the word in bold in the first column. These are **synonyms** which are words with a similar meaning.

1.	**bramble**	tree	(thorn)	bulb	berry
2.	**stem**	petal	lead	(stalk)	shoot
3.	**grow**	tall	(fertilise)	seed	cultivate
4.	**shrub**	destroy	(bush)	soil	tree
5.	**vegetable**	(produce)	diet	plant	fruit
6.	**grain**	grass	fern	(seed)	bark
7.	**creeper**	tower	root	healthy	(vine)
8.	**twig**	trunk	(sprig)	leaf	harvest

F Put these **verbs** in the correct order to show the process by which plants grow and define each one. The last is done for you.

sprout	blossom	plant	**seed**	germinate	die

1. Verb: _sprout is_ Definition: _is to a plant growing_

2. Verb: _plant is_ Definition: _is to plant a seed_

3. Verb: _die is_ Definition: _means to stop existing_

4. Verb: _blossom is_ Definition: _to the petals opening up_

5. Verb: _germinate is_ Definition: _to grow the shoots_

6. Verb: *seed* Definition: *new seed appears for next growth*

Weather

A Which weather group do these words belong to? Add them to the chart in the right **classification** group. Two of the words are a match for 2 groups – highlight them .

flood	sleet	thunder	slush
frost	thaw	rainbow	lightning
gale	drought	tornado	icicle
flake	cyclone	heatwave	flurry

snow	wind	rain
slush flake thaw	tornado cyclone sleet	rainbow thunder flurry

sun	ice
heatwave drought rainbow	icicle thaw frost

B Weather is often included in descriptions. To compare weather to other times and places, we use **comparatives and superlatives**. Complete this chart to show these. One is done for you. Remember we sometimes use 'more' for comparatives and 'most' for superlatives.

adjective	comparative	superlative
cold	*colder*	*coldest*
1. hot	hotter	hottest
2. chilly	chillier	chilliest
3. refreshing	refreshinger	refreshingest
4. damp	damper	dampest
5. clear	clearer	clearest
6. strong	stronger	strongest

C Identify the word closest in meaning to the bold word in the first column. Look up the words in a dictionary if you are unsure.

1.	**fog**	hail	gale	blast	(mist)
2.	**cyclone**	cold	hurricane	(destruction)	earthquake
3.	**storm**	thunder	drizzle	(tempest)	front
4.	**boiling**	sunshine	(blazing)	blaring	temperature
5.	**windy**	(breezy)	bleak	overcast	rainy
6.	**snowslide**	flurry	mountain	(slope)	avalanche

D Make the passage make sense by adding the correct words to the **cloze** passage. Each word can only be used once so highlight or cross out each one as you use it.

temperature	forecast	Fahrenheit	sunshine	wind
rain	freezing	Celsius	degrees	weather

After the news, there will always be a **1.** _weather_ report which gives you

information about what the next day will be like. They will tell you how hot or cold

it is by giving details of the **2.** _temperature_ and this is shown by how many

3. _degrees_ it is. This measurement can be shown using either **4.** _celsius_

or **5.** _Farenheit_ . If it gets to 0 °C, this is known as the **6.** _freezing_ point.

Lines are used on the maps to show the direction of the **7.** _wind_ . The weather

reporters also use symbols to show the weather **8.** _forecast_ for different areas

of the country. These are simple images of types of weather like **9.** _rain_ and

10. _sunshine_ .

E Combine words to make **compound words**. You can use a word more than once but try to use every word. See if you can make 10 compound words.

bathe	rain	hail
sun	flake	storm
cloud	bolt	thunder
snow	burn	bow

sunbathe   sunburn

raincloud   snowstorm

snowflake   hailstorm

thunderstorm   thundercloud

thunderbolt   rainstorm

Words within Words

A The word **meteorology** is used to describe weather and weather conditions. The word 'meteor' refers to things 'high up' and '-logy' is used for 'study' so it means 'studying things high up'.

How many words can you make out of the word 'meteorological'?
Use a timer or someone to compete against to make it more interesting. You could get 2 points for any words connected to the weather or 5 for words of more letters.

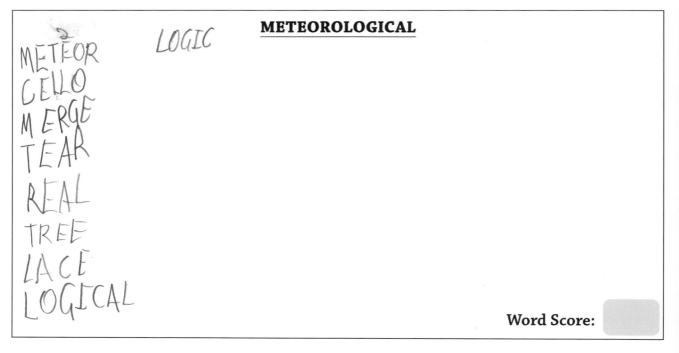

METEOROLOGICAL

LOGIC

METEOR
CELLO
MERGE
TEAR
REAL
TREE
LACE
LOGICAL

Word Score:

B The word **amphibians** is used to describe animals which can live on the land and in water. They are cold-blooded, but do not have scales like reptiles.

How many words can you make out of the word 'amphibians'?
Use a timer or someone to compete against to make it more interesting. You could get 2 points for any words connected to the animals or 5 for words of more letters.

AMPHIBIANS

PAIN   NAB
PAINS   SNAB

S PAIN
SNAP
BAN
PI
BIN

Word Score:

HUMANS

Body Matters

A There are 6 body parts jumbled up here. Pair up the words which refer to the same body part by drawing lines between them or colour coding. These pairs of words are **synonyms**.

chest	jaw *3*
leg	back *5*
chin	mind *4*
brain	torso *1*
spine	limb *2*

B Put the face back together again by working out which words form part of these areas of the face. Add them to the correct **classification** column. Look up any you do not know in a dictionary.

lips	pupil	tongue	smell	lobe	iris	septum
taste	lash	nostril	lid	nasal cavity	canal	drum
brow	sight	lens	bridge	gum	teeth	tonsils

ear	nose	mouth	eye
canal drum bridge	smell nosh nasal cavity lobe septum	lips tongue teeth gum tonsls taste	lens lid iris pupil sight lash brow

C We have many words for talking and walking in English. Although these words are often **synonyms**, they do not mean exactly the same. Your challenge here is to find the word *most similar in meaning* to the first **word** so think very carefully about all the 'talk' and 'walk' options.

1.	whisper	(murmur)	declare	stammer	challenge
2.	shout	tell	chant	(yell)	call
3.	cry	slur	(weep)	announce	state
4.	argue	stutter	chatter	tell	(disagree)
5.	stroll	saunter	limp	(shuffle)	plod
6.	march	plod	prance	toddle	(parade)
7.	stumble	step	(hobble)	tiptoe	run
8.	wander	turn	trip	(roam)	skip

D Choose *one word from each set of brackets* to complete the sentence. Underline or highlight the words. The sentence will only make sense if the **word connection** is the same for each half of the sentence.

1. Eye is to (**see**, glasses, pupil) as ear is to (drum, loud, **hear**).

2. Thigh is to (bone, break, **leg**) as elbow is to (**arm**, poke, bend).

3. Heart is to (live, **pump**, large) as stomach is to (hungry, food, **digest**).

4. Height is to (metre, short, **measure**) as weight is to (food, **kilo**, wait).

5. Finger is to (thumb, touch, **hand**) as toe is to (ankle, **foot**, nail).

6. Drink is to (water, liquid, **thirst**) as food is to (**hunger**, eat, cook).

E In these sentences there are **missing 3-letter words**.
Write out the words which will complete the spelling of the words in capitals.

1. People who are really ill have to go to **HOSAL**.

2. A fever can cause a high **TEMPEURE**.

3. Our **SKEONS** are made up of all our bones.

4. Food passes into our **INTESES** to be digested.

5. If we break a bone, it is called a **FRURE**.

6. **BIOY** is the study of living things.

HOSPITAL
TEMPRATURE
SKELETONS
INTESTINES
FRACTURE
BIOLOGY

F Look at these **body words** and select the right ones to answer the questions below. Look up words which you do not know.

tibia	vein
digit	fever
femur	artery
wrist	canine
lung	molar
liver	swelling

1. Which two carry blood in the body? _____ *vein* _____ and _____ *artery* _____

2. Which two are leg bones? _____ *femur* _____ and _____ *digit* _____

3. Which two are internal organs? _____ *lung* _____ and _____ *liver* _____

4. Which two are parts of the arm? _____ *wrist* _____ and _____ *tibia* _____

5. Which two suggest an infection? _____ *swelling* _____ and _____ *fever* _____

6. Which two are types of teeth? _____ *molar* _____ and _____ *canine* _____

Dressing Up

A Some of these clothes and accessories words are **homographs**. This means they have more than one meaning.

The words belong to 2 different word classes, a verb and a noun. Identify the 3 words below which are homographs and write out the 2 different definitions for them.

suit	gown	blouse	scarf
hat	coat	dress	trousers

1. **First homograph:** _Suit_

   Meaning 1: _Suit you   war_

   Meaning 2: _Suits you_

2. **Second homograph:** _Coat_

   Meaning 1: _Coat you wear_

   Meaning 2: _loads of coats_

3. **Third homograph:** _Dress_

   Meaning 1: _dress you   wear_

   Meaning 2: _dressing someone_

B Sort out the words into **classifications**. On which part of the body would you wear them?

turtleneck	sarong	slipper	poncho
moccasin	visor	tutu	mule
balaclava	blouse	trunks	jodhpurs
sombrero	kilt	hoodie	anorak

top	bottom
hoodie ponchos sarong blouse	kilt jodhpurs

head	bottom
balaclava sombrero	slipper

C Look at these **jumbled sentences** and write them out correctly. One word is not needed.

1. **freezing of hat woolly in she snow spite and her was scarf.**

   Full sentence: _____

   Extra word: _____

2. **outfits wear to dance school rules they to new bought the**

   Full sentence: _____

   Extra word: _____

3. **wool made silk design be cotton of kaftans can or**

   Full sentence: _____

   Extra word: _____

4. **ceremony many to veils choose traditionally brides have long**

   Full sentence: _____

   Extra word: _____

D Which 2 words are the **odd ones out** in each line? Highlight or circle them.

1.	cap	gloves	beret	scarf	turban
2.	umbrella	parka	anorak	duffle	gown
3.	slipper	loafer	sandal	sneaker	sock
4.	satchel	backpack	trunk	trolley	handbag
5.	earring	armband	ring	bracelet	bangle
6.	wear	show	dress	carry	clothe

E Can you put these clothes back together by pairing them up to make compound **words**? Link them by lines or colour coding.

track	gown
rain	scarf
sun	coat
neck	suit
head	glasses
night	tie

F The word **accessory** is used to describe items we might add to an outfit to make it look better or to be useful in some way. Which 3 of these words are **synonyms** of the word accessory?

decoration	adornment	establishment
indication	embellishment	arrangement

Sport

A Choose one word from each set of brackets to complete the sentence. Underline or highlight the words.

The sentence will only make sense if the **word relationship** is the same for each half of the sentence.

Tip: some are **homophones**.

1. Cricket is to (**ball, run, bat**) as tennis is to (**score, racquet, net**).
2. Caught is to (**clap, court, cross**) as exercise is to (**exclude, exclaim, exorcise**).
3. Football is to (**goal, post, score**) as basketball is to (**jump, point, high**).
4. Weight is to (**kilo, measure, wait**) as cue is to (**queue, snooker, ball**).
5. Pool is to (**swimming, water, compete**) as pitch is to (**size, football, last**).
6. Golf is to (**club, green, shirt**) as hockey is to (**injury, stick, player**).

B Each of these sport and exercise words are **homographs**. For each one, write out the 2 definitions. Some are nouns for both but some can be a noun and a verb.

1. **train**

   Meaning 1: _____

   Meaning 2: _____

2. **fit**

   Meaning 1: _____

   Meaning 2: _____

3. **row**

   Meaning 1: _____

   Meaning 2: _____

4. **record**

   Meaning 1: _____

   Meaning 2: _____

5. **bat**

   Meaning 1: _____

   Meaning 2: _____

6. **play**

   Meaning 1: _____

   Meaning 2: _____

C In these sentences there are missing 3-letter words. Identify the sports to find them. Write out the words which will complete the spelling of the sport.

1. You need a bow and arrow to do **ARCY.**   _____

2. There are lots of events in **ATHICS.**   _____

3. We use a shuttlecock in **BADMIN.**   _____

4. **KAE** is a martial arts sport.   _____

5. A popular sport among skiers is **SBOARDING.**   _____

6. Jumping out of planes is called **PARACING.**   _____

D Complete the following **cloze passage** by writing in the correct words. Each one can only be used once, so cross them out or highlight them to eliminate them as you use them.

impact	organs	interaction	physical	trophies	mental
confidence	league	participate	exercise	skills	team

Sports provide opportunities for everyone to **1.** _____, whatever their age or gender. There are lots of **2.** _____ activities available to suit anybody and taking part has many advantages.

Obviously, doing any kind of **3.** _____ will have a positive **4.** _____ on your health. Regular exercise will benefit all your **5.** _____ but especially your heart. As well as this, sport also helps with your **6.** _____ health because it can build up your **7.** _____ about what you can achieve.

Finally, sport is very good for team-building **8.** _____ as you have to work with others to be successful. This involves social **9.** _____ with others, so joining a

10. _____ could lead to new friendships as well as the opportunity to win

11. _____ and come top of the **12.** _____.

E Identify the **antonyms** by finding the word most *opposite in meaning* to the word in bold in the first column.

1.	**winner**	last	fair	loser	competition
2.	**interact**	isolate	team	give	play
3.	**bend**	turn	bow	twist	straighten
4.	**idle**	winner	active	sort	league
5.	**failure**	loss	sad	cup	success
6.	**throw**	catch	sling	try	ball
7.	**break**	leg	mend	bandage	injury
8.	**support**	together	health	hinder	help

Words within Words

A **How many words can you make out of the word 'accessories'?**
Use a timer or someone to compete against to make it more interesting. You could get 2 points for any words connected to dressing or words of 5 or more letters.

<u>**ACCESSORIES**</u>

Word Score:

B **How many words can you make out of the word 'participation'?**
Use a timer or someone to compete against to make it more interesting. You could get 2 points for any words connected to sport or activity or words of 5 or more letters.

<u>**PARTICIPATION**</u>

Word Score:

ART, HISTORY AND LITERATURE

Painting and Drawing

A Sort these colour words into the correct **classification** by writing them in the chart below. Highlight or cross them out as you go to help you work out what is left. There should be 4 words for each colour. Look up any you do not know.

ruby	olive	emerald	lemon	amber	navy	turquoise	sand
azure	crimson	gold	teal	sage	lime	scarlet	cherry

blue	red	green	yellow

B Which word is the *closest in meaning* to the bold word in the first column? Circle or highlight it. A word with a similar meaning is a **synonym**.

1.	**illustrate**	show	decorate	sculpt	write
2.	**copy**	share	photo	design	reproduce
3.	**painting**	colourful	brush	picture	frame
4.	**artist**	painter	expert	famous	gallery
5.	**mix**	double	combine	together	rainbow
6.	**sketch**	fade	detail	draw	pencil
7.	**shade**	lamp	chalk	colour	dark
8.	**sculpture**	carving	person	pot	garden

C Can you solve the mystery of these **jumbled up** art words? The definitions should help you work out what the right order for these words is. Spell each correctly.

1. A **SCIMAO** is a pattern of tiles, stones or glass. _____

2. **MIAGRIO** is making objects out of paper. _____

3. **XELETTI** is a word which means material. _____

4. Artists mix paint on a **LETAPTE**. _____

5. **KLCAH** is used to write on a blackboard. _____

6. A **NILSTESOLEA** is a pattern of fitted shapes. _____

7. We can visit a **LGYALRE** to see paintings. _____

8. A **LGCLAOE** is art made from cut-up pictures. _____

D Pair up the words to make these artistic **compound words**. Choose one from each column. Write them out below.

paint	colour
out	lap
water	line
brush	brush
over	stroke

1. compound word: _____   **2.** compound word: _____

3. compound word: _____   **4.** compound word: _____

5. compound word: _____

E Which 2 words are the **odd ones out** in each line? Highlight or circle them.

1.	picture	face	portrait	figure	drawing
2.	technique	shade	tone	line	colour
3.	ceramic	pottery	stoneware	cup	kiln
4.	special	contrast	similarity	difference	variation
5.	scenery	countryside	bush	landscape	tree
6.	background	line	stroke	perspective	mark

F ROYGBIV is used by many people to remember the order of the colours of the rainbow. Do you know them all? Fill in ROYGBIV below and draw a rainbow in this order underneath.

1. R _____

2. O _____

3. Y _____

4. G _____

5. B _____

6. I _____

7. V _____

rainbow

Power and Conquest

A Identify the words closest in meaning for these words which are used to discuss historical events. Highlight or ring the correct **synonym** for the word in bold.

1.	**invention**	wind	creation	draw	machine
2.	**evidence**	proof	time	document	find
3.	**civilisation**	governor	rule	kind	culture
4.	**artefact**	truth	artist	object	coin
5.	**chronology**	grey	metal	order	early
6.	**ancient**	ruined	fast	pyramid	old
7.	**source**	reference	water	study	create
8.	**era**	long	period	mistake	last

B Match up these Viking words to their **definitions**.

fjord	navigate	warrior	runes	Norse	hoard	seafaring	plunder

1. fighter in battle   _____
2. letters or symbols in an alphabet   _____
3. stealing property in wartime   _____
4. Norwegian language   _____
5. store of valuable items   _____
6. steer and direct the course of a ship   _____
7. regularly travels by sea   _____
8. narrow inlet from the sea with cliffs   _____

C Turn these verbs into **people nouns**. For example, 'fight' will become 'fighter'. Remember the ending could be 'er' or 'or'.

1. A person who 'invents' is an _____.
2. A person who 'explores' is a _____.
3. A person who 'rules' is a _____.
4. A person who 'dictates' is a _____.
5. A person who 'settles' is a _____.
6. A person who 'invades' is an _____.
7. A person who 'survives' is a _____.
8. A person who 'conquers' is a _____.

CHALLENGE

What do we call someone who betrays others? It starts with 't'.

_____

D Building castles: the incomplete words in capitals spell out parts of a castle. In each, there is a **missing word** of 2 or 3 letters. Use the definitions to help you work out both the complete word and the 2/3-letter word.

Find the 3-letter words.

1. **BATTLETS** – at the top of the castle.

   Complete word: _____ Missing word: _____

2. **GHOUSE** – entrance to the castle.

   Complete word: _____ Missing word: _____

3. **DRAWBGE** – used to cross the moat.

   Complete word: _____ Missing word: _____

Find the 2-letter words.

4. **FTRESS** – another name for castle.

   Complete word: _____ Missing word: _____

5. **MO** – water round the castle.

   Complete word: _____ Missing word: _____

6. **BNER** – flag flying over the castle.

   Complete word: _____ Missing word: _____

E The **suffix** '-ology' means 'study' so when we add it to a word, it means the study of something. In history, 'archaeology' is the study of the remains of human life such as pottery and tools and ruins. Can you match these words to what they study?

zoology	birds
astrology	society
psychology	star signs
ecology	mind
sociology	animals
ornithology	environment

F Sort these people into 3 **classifications**: *working classes, nobility and rulers* by writing W, N or R next to them or by colour coding.

sir	serf	baron	domestic	lord
dictator	lady	emperor	king	president
servant	monarch	labourer	peasant	farmhand
duchess	earl	aristocrat	duke	queen

Writers and Forms of Writing

A Who writes what? For each **form of writing**, write the word we use to describe a person who writes that form. Be careful to spell each word correctly.

1. A word to describe any person who publishes writing is an **a** _____.

2. A person who writes *poems* is called a _____.

3. A person who writes *novels* is called a _____.

4. A person who writes *plays* is called a _____.

5. A person who writes *biographies* is called a _____.

6. A person who writes *for a newspaper* is called a _____.

B Can you solve the mystery of these **jumbled up** book words? They are all words which describe a part of a book. Spell each correctly.

1. The OERCV is the outside of a book. _____

2. The LTETI is the name of a book. _____

3. A SNOCNTET page tells you what is in the book. _____

4. The SLRSGAOY defines words. _____

5. The LBRBU is on the back of the book. _____

6. The IPESN of a book can be seen on a bookshelf. _____

C Match up the words on the left with those on the right to make **compound words**. They are all about writers and writing. Draw lines or colour code to link them.

foot	storm
form	paper
cross	line
back	at
dead	pad
news	stage
key	note
brain	word

Extension: 'book' can make a lot of compound words. See if you can make 6.

1. book_____ 2. book_____

3. book_____ 4. book_____

5. book_____ 6. book_____

D Choose one word from each set of brackets to complete the sentence. Underline or highlight the words. The sentence will only make sense if the **word relationship** is the same for each half of the sentence.

1. Story is to (**read, tail, tale**) as playwright is to (**stage, dramatist, theatre**).

2. Poet is to (**rhyme, poem, song**) as journalist is to (**article, office, event**).

3. Cinema is to (**show, film, watch**) as theatre is to (**run, ticket, play**).

4. Read is to (**book, grass, study**) as listen is to (**ear, radio, hear**).

5. Detective is to (**crime, solve, criminal**) as hero is to (**villain, win, heroine**).

6. Narrate is to (**tell, finish, judge**) as persuade is to (**convince, argue, show**).

E Match these **genres** of fiction to their definitions below.

sci-fi	myth	gothic	western
fantasy	spy	fable	crime

1. These stories feature ghosts, secrets and scary locations. _____

2. You often find animals in these and they teach lessons. _____

3. These stories might include codes and be set in wartime. _____

4. There are always cowboys and horses in these stories. _____

5. These contain gods and often explain things in nature. _____

6. These are set in the future and on other planets. _____

7. Look out for detectives who want to catch villains. _____

8. Stories like these have strange creatures and lands. _____

F Many of Shakespeare's sayings have become part of everyday language. See if you can finish these **idioms**. The first letter is given.

1. The boy had *vanished into thin a_____*.

2. *All that glistens is not g_____*.

3. You can *have too much of a g_____ thing*.

4. She was very open and *wore her h_____ upon her sleeve*.

5. Jealousy is *the green-eyed m_____*.

6. My grandmother has *a h_____ of gold*.

7. *In the t_____ of an eye*, she had disappeared.

8. The salesman refused to *budge an i_____* on the price.

27

Words within Words

A **How many words can you make out of the word 'archaeology'?**

Use a timer or someone to compete against to make it more interesting. You could get 2 points for any words connected to history or 5 for words of more letters.

ARCHAEOLOGY

Word Score:

B **How many words can you make out of the word 'literature'?**

Give yourself double marks for every word about writing or books and for words of 5 or more letters.

LITERATURE

Word Score:

SCIENCE AND TECHNOLOGY

Transport

A Sort these transport methods into the correct **classification** – air, land or water.

coach	balloon	hovercraft	liner
yacht	glider	tram	helicopter
space shuttle	ferry	scooter	gondola
moped	dinghy	airship	truck

air	land	water

B Use the **code** to work out the names of these types of transport.

A	B	C	D	E	F	G	H	I	J	K	L	M
1	2	3	4	5	6	7	8	9	10	11	12	13

N	O	P	Q	R	S	T	U	V	W	X	Y	Z
14	15	16	17	18	19	20	21	22	23	24	25	26

1. 22-1-14 _____

2. 7-12-9-4-5-18 _____

3. 25-1-3-8-20 _____

4. 20-18-1-9-14 _____

5. 3-1-18-1-22-1-14 _____

6. 2-9-3-25-3-12-5 _____

C These **jumbled up words** are words to describe parts of a boat. Unjumble them.

1. The LUHL is the outer part of a boat. _____

2. The back of a boat is the RSNTE. _____

3. An HOACNR stops a boat from moving. _____

4. The SAMT is the upright post on a ship. _____

5. A small window is a HTOEPLOR. _____

6. A RLITLE is used to steer a boat. _____

D Which word is the *closest in meaning* to the bold word in the first column? Circle or highlight these speed words. A word with a similar meaning is a **synonym**.

1.	**accelerate**	hill	decelerate	quicken	press
2.	**limit**	join	capacity	force	turn
3.	**distance**	length	breadth	width	height
4.	**velocity**	speed	mile	time	repeat
5.	**rapid**	further	careful	water	fast
6.	**transport**	road	vehicle	track	lane
7.	**decelerate**	stop	wheel	slow	steer
8.	**ascend**	descend	climb	slope	improve

E Complete the **compound words** by choosing from the options.

shield	craft	cab	boat
park	port	belt	way

1. taxi _____

2. wind _____

3. life _____

4. hover _____

5. seat _____

6. car _____

7. motor _____ and high _____ – use the same word for both.

8. pass _____ and air _____ – use the same word for both.

F Complete the following **cloze passage** by writing in the correct words. Each one can only be used once, so cross them out or highlight them to eliminate them after you have used them.

horses	transportation	leisure	foot	goods
century	camels	aeroplane	steam	wheel

In the earliest days, people had to travel on **1.** _____ and use animals like

2. _____ and **3.** _____ to carry things. A really important invention from

over 5000 years ago was the **4.** _____. This simple object made moving things so

much easier and is essential for most forms of **5.** _____ today.

Another important invention in the eighteenth **6.** _____ was the **7.** _____

engine. The railways enabled huge quantities of **8.** _____ to be transported and

allowed people to travel for **9.** _____.

In the early part of the twentieth century, the Wright brothers designed and flew the

first **10.** _____ which transformed the time it took to travel to other places.

The Environment

A Choose one word from each set of brackets to complete the sentence. Underline or highlight the words. The sentence will only make sense if the **word relationship** is the same for each half of the sentence.

1. Waste is to (**food, recycle, bin**) as endanger is to (**scary, find, protect**).

2. Wind is to (**typhoon, blow, cold**) as rain is to (**water, flood, coat**).

3. Conserve is to (**know, face, save**) as fumes are to (**gases, strong, fire**).

4. Animal is to (**play, wildlife, alive**) as tree is to (**forest, leaf, branch**).

5. Climate is to (**weather, sun, dark**) as global is to (**big, sphere, world**).

6. Grow is to (**plant, die, earth**) as warm is to (**heat, cool, abroad**).

B Match the words with each other to create well-known **phrases** to do with the environment. Draw lines or use colour coding.

eco	layer
oil	energy
rain	system
renewable	warming
ozone	slick
global	forest

C Which 2 words are the **odd ones out** in each line? Highlight or circle them.

1.	rest	recycle	renew	reward	reclaim
2.	effect	pollute	solar	impact	consequence
3.	orangutan	jaguar	chimpanzee	gorilla	parrot
4.	violet	green	sand	emerald	lime
5.	pollute	purify	poison	clean	contaminate
6.	package	litter	refuse	rubbish	plastic

D Consider how the **prefixes** 'de' and 're' are used when discussing the environment. 'De' means *reducing or taking away* so is often seen as negative, while 're' means *again or more* so is normally positive. Add 're' or 'de' to these words.

_____-cover   _____-new   _____-claim

_____-compose   _____-forestation   _____-fresh

_____-crease   _____-plant   _____-grade

_____-frost   _____-store   _____-cycle

E Find the **hidden 4-letter word** in this sentence. It will use letters from the end of one word and the start of the next. Look carefully between each pair of words and write out the word when you find it.

1. Wind power is a renewable and cost-effective source of energy.

    4-letter word: _____

2. You can be a climate ambassador by educating others about recycling.

    4-letter word: _____

3. If pollution ceased, the planet would last many more years.

    4-letter word: _____

4. The rainforest operates with a unique ecosystem.

    4-letter word: _____

5. Experts in drought estimate that global warming will make this worse.

    4-letter word: _____

6. Global solar energy would solve many climate problems.

    4-letter word: _____

F **Etymology** is a word we use for the study of words and where they come from. Often, they come from Greek or Latin words. See if you can match up the words and their meanings. Use colour coding or lines to connect the pairs.

energy	'from the sun'
global	'productive or fruitful'
ecology	'work or activity'
solar	'keeping the same'
conservation	'all the world'
fertile	'study of where you live'

Earth and Sky

A We often use **mnemonics** to help us remember lists of words. There are many to help us with the planets. Use this one to help you get them in order and remember to give them all a capital letter.

Mnemonic	Planets
My	
very	
easy	
method	
just	
speeds	
up	
naming	
(planets).	**Pluto** used to be here but was removed as a planet in 2006.

B Find the **missing 3-letter word** which completes the word in capitals

1. **JUER** is the largest planet in the solar system. _____

2. An **ECSE** can make day appear to be night. _____

3. A **TELESE** can help you see for miles. _____

4. The Earth's **ATMOSPE** surrounds our planet. _____

5. Earth's **MOVET** round the sun takes a year. _____

6. **SATELES** revolve around bigger objects. _____

7. The earth **ROES** on its axis. _____

8. In a **PLAARIUM** you can see the Milky Way. _____

C Pair up the space words to create **compound words**. Use lines or colour coding to link the two halves.

super	beam
space	length
star	craft
wave	dial
moon	dust
sun	nova

D Match these space words to their **definitions** below. Write them out.

eclipse	gravity	observatory	satellite
constellation	rocket	meteorite	orbit

1. a group of stars _____

2. a space craft _____

3. a place to watch the sky _____

4. force or pull of the earth _____

5. blocking the moon or sun _____

6. path followed by an object _____

7. stone or metal falling _____

8. something moving round an object _____

E Identify the word closest in meaning to the bold word in the first column. This will be a **synonym**.

1.	**orbit**	round	speed	path	little
2.	**atmosphere**	breathe	air	pull	liquid
3.	**rotate**	reverse	climb	rodent	turn
4.	**eclipse**	cover	moon	cold	repeat
5.	**phase**	word	stage	past	fade
6.	**lunar**	light	dark	sun	moon
7.	**space**	planet	galaxy	star	outer
8.	**alien**	strange	kind	monster	spare

F Complete the cloze passage about gravity using the words in the box.

Earth	force	space	sun	ground
planets	Newton	gravity	football	weightless

Sir Isaac **1.** _____ discovered the idea of **2.** _____ .

This is the pull or **3.** _____ which makes things fall to the **4.** _____ like a

5. _____ after being kicked up in the air.

Gravity is what keeps the **6.** _____ in its place so it can continue to orbit around the

7. _____ and other **8.** _____ also remain stable. Without it, we and all the

objects on earth would become **9.** _____ and float around **10.** _____ .

Words within Words

A **How many words can you make from 'environment'?**

Time yourself or compete with a friend. Score 2 points for every word which is about the environment or 5 for words of more letters.

ENVIRONMENT

Word Score:

B **How many words can you make from 'transportation'?**

Time yourself or compete with a friend. Score 2 points for every word which is about the environment or 5 for words of more letters.

TRANSPORTATION

Word Score:

MATHEMATICS, MONEY AND REASONING

Area and Shape

A These shapes all have a different **number of sides**. By looking at the first part of each word, identify how many each has and write them out below.

hexagon	nonagon	octagon
heptagon	pentagon	decagon

1. 5 sides _____

2. 6 sides _____

3. 7 sides _____

4. 8 sides _____

5. 9 sides _____

6. 10 sides _____

B For each of the **prefixes** in bold, identify the meaning out of the choices. Highlight or circle the right answer.

1.	semi-	half	quarter	bit
2.	cent-	ten	past	hundred
3.	ir-	wrong	not	before
4.	uni-	whole	one	first
5.	mega-	thousand	hundred	huge
6.	tri-	last	third	three

C Match the shape terms to their **definitions**. Write them out.

vertex	area	angle	diameter
perimeter	circumference	side	volume

1. measured in degrees _____

2. the edge of a shape _____

3. measure of the surface of a shape _____

4. distance across a circle _____

5. space taken up by a 3D shape _____

6. a point where faces meet _____

7. distance around a shape _____

8. the outside of a circle _____

D Use the **code** to work out the names of these 2D and 3D shapes.

A	B	C	D	E	F	G	H	I	J	K	L	M
1	2	3	4	5	6	7	8	9	10	11	12	13

N	O	P	Q	R	S	T	U	V	W	X	Y	Z
14	15	16	17	18	19	20	21	22	23	24	25	26

1. 11-9-20-5 _____

2. 3-9-18-3-12-5 _____

3. 3-21-2-5 _____

4. 19-16-8-5-18-5 _____

5. 20-18-9-1-14-7-12-5 _____

6. 16-25-18-1-13-9-4 _____

7. 19-17-21-1-18-5 _____

8. 15-3-20-1-7-15-14 _____

E Sort these words into the correct **classification** group in the chart below.

circle	cone	volume
pyramid	diameter	triangle
area	sphere	cube
parallelogram	rectangle	angle

2 dimensional shapes	3 dimensional shapes	shape measurements

F All of these shape words have been used in this section. Can you complete them with the missing **3-letter word**. It must be spelt correctly.

1. PERI _____ ER

2. PEN _____ ON

3. PY _____ ID

4. DI _____ SIONAL

5. REC _____ GLE

6. SH _____ S

39

Numbers

A Highlight or ring the word *closest in meaning* to the bold word in the first column. A word with a similar meaning is a **synonym**.

1.	**add**	plus	more	equal
2.	**subtract**	less	under	minus
3.	**equivalent**	share	same	length
4.	**multiply**	many	clock	times
5.	**estimate**	guess	approximate	friend
6.	**divide**	share	remove	score
7.	**remainder**	important	stay	leftover
8.	**fraction**	part	broken	perform

B Complete the sentences with the correct words to match the **definitions**.

numerator	ratio
fraction	factor
prime	integer
multiple	denominator

1. _____ is used to describe a number only divisible by 1 and itself.

2. _____ is the value on the bottom of a fraction.

3. _____ is a whole number.

4. _____ compares 2 numbers.

5. _____ is the top number of a fraction.

6. _____ is a number which divides into another number exactly.

7. _____ is a way of showing part of a whole number.

8. _____ refers to all numbers which are part of that times table.

C Find the **hidden 4-letter word** in this sentence. It will use letters from the end of one word and the start of the next. Look carefully between each pair of words and write out the word when you find it.

1. You can work out an approximate amount by rounding up or down.

   4-letter word: _____

2. When we do mental mathematics, we work out sums in our heads.

   4-letter word: _____

3. Often division is easier if you do the opposite operation of multiplication.

4-letter word: _____

4. Now educated people know three quarters is seventy-five percent.

4-letter word: _____

D Find one word or figure from each set of brackets to complete the sentence. Underline or highlight the words or figures.
The sentence will only make sense if the **word relationship** is the same for each half of the sentence.

1. Add is to (**count, subtract**) as multiply is to (**divide, improve**).

2. Correct is to (**right, green**) as estimate is to (**add, approximate**).

3. Twelve is to (**digits, months**) as fifty-two is to (**weeks, days**).

4. Half is to (**whole, quarter**) as 50% is to (**100%, 80%**).

5. One third is to (**four sixths, 5 sixths**) as two eighths is to (**a half, a quarter**).

6. 9 is to (**27, 81**) as 7 is to (**28, 49**).

E Fit the numbers into the **cloze passage** in the correct places.

7	24	365	28	60	29	52	12

The Gregorian calendar is used almost everywhere in the world and is based on how many days it takes for the Earth to orbit the sun which is **1.** _____ days. This is split into **2.** _____ calendar months. The shortest month has only **3.** _____ days but this becomes **4.** _____ every four years and these are called leap years.

Months can be broken down further into weeks, of which there are **5.** _____ in a year. The week can then be viewed as **6.** _____ days. Each day is split into **7.** _____ hours and each hour is then divided into **8.** _____ minutes.

F To compare numbers to each other, it is useful to use comparatives and superlatives. Complete this chart by filling in the **comparatives and superlatives** for the words in the first column. Sometimes you may need to use 'more' for a comparative or 'most' for a superlative. Some are irregular.

	adjective	comparative	superlative
1.	far		
2.	great		
3.	easy		
4.	difficult		
5.	expensive		
6.	little		

Statistics

A Identify these charts which are used to present statistics. Match them to their **definitions.**

venn diagram	bar graph	pictogram
line graph	pie chart	table

1. A _____ is used to organise raw data so we can see it easily.

2. A _____ uses pictures to represent the data.

3. A _____ uses columns or blocks.

4. A _____ uses a circle split into segments to show percentages.

5. A _____ uses a line to show how data changes over time.

6. A _____ overlaps circles which each show groups of data.

B Complete each word in bold by adding a **3-letter word**. The words are all to do with statistics so use the definitions to help you.

1. The **AVE_____E** is the mean of something.

2. We present **IN_____MATION** in a chart.

3. A **S_____TER** diagram shows information with a series of dots.

4. A **DIAG_____** is a way of presenting statistics visually.

5. We can find out information by conducting a **QUESTIONN_____E.**

6. Charts allow us to make **COM_____ISONS** between groups of data.

C 3 of these words are **homographs**. Identify which words are homographs and write out the 2 meanings for each. For some, the meanings will be 2 nouns but the second may be a verb so look carefully.

bar	graph	compare
median	plot	form

1. **Homograph 1:** _____

   Meaning 1: _____

   Meaning 2: _____

2. **Homograph 2:** _____

   Meaning 1: _____

   Meaning 2: _____

3. **Homograph 3:** _____

   Meaning 1: _____

   Meaning 2: _____

D In these **jumbled up sentences** one word is not needed. Write them out correctly and identified the extra word.

1. **score the is middle median last the.**

   Correct sentence: _____

   Extra word: _____

2. **calculate data can graph ordering mode we by.**

   Correct sentence: _____

   Extra word: _____

3. **section a is the population of choose sample a.**

   Correct sentence: _____

   Extra word: _____

E Use a table or chart to help you work out the answers to this **word problem**.

Four children take their pocket money to a sweet shop. Joni buys sherbet lemons, chocolate and flying saucers. Claudia has the same but has cola cubes instead of flying saucers. Benjy buys sherbet lemons, lollipops and flying saucers while Ali gets sherbet lemons and lollipops.

1. Which are the most popular sweets? _____

2. Which is the least popular sweet? _____

3. Who has the least sweets? _____

4. Which 2 children have flying saucers? _____

5. Which 2 children have lollipops? _____

F Use the **coding** chart below to help work out the statistics words below.

A	B	C	D	E	F	G	H	I	J	K	L	M
1	2	3	4	5	6	7	8	9	10	11	12	13

N	O	P	Q	R	S	T	U	V	W	X	Y	Z
14	15	16	17	18	19	20	21	22	23	24	25	26

1. 4-1-20-1 _____

2. 1-22-5-18-1-7-5 _____

3. 16-9-3-20-15-7-18-1-13 _____

4. 20-1-2-12-5 _____

5. 13-5-4-9-1-14 _____

Words within Words

A **How many words can you make from 'parallelogram'?**

Time yourself or compete with a friend. Double your points for every word which is about mathematics or 5 for words of more letters.

PARALLELOGRAM
Word Score:

B **How many words can you make from 'questionnaire'?**

Time yourself or compete with a friend. Double your points for every word which is about statistics or 5 for words of more letters.

QUESTIONNAIRE
Word Score:

GRAMMAR
VOCABULARY

Word Classes

A Change the word class of each of these words from **adjectives to adverbs**. The first one is done for you.

adjective	adverb
quick	*quickly*
1. happy	
2. slow	
3. painful	
4. sad	
5. terrible	
6. hopeful	
7. fast	
8. joyful	

B Pair up the **prepositions** with their opposite counterpart by colour coding or drawing lines between them.

with	above	after	towards
including	away	inside	beneath
before	outside	without	excluding

C Insert the correct **relative pronoun** into each of these sentences. Choose from the options given. You may use them more than once.

whose	which	when	whom	where	who

1. My mother said she would call me _____ it was time to come indoors.

2. Gerry passed the ball to the girl _____ was playing on the left wing.

3. The family, _____ mother worked at the school, stayed later.

4. They forfeited the match _____ should have been played that weekend.

5. We all longed to go back to the island _____ we had holidayed last year.

6. The teacher _____ she had last year, had left the school.

7. Freya spotted the sweets _____ she adored.

8. The swimming coach, _____ name was Levi, lined them all up.

9. Everyone decided to go to the park _____ school had finished.

10. The girl _____ I sat next to was really funny and friendly.

Prefixes

A Prefixes change the meaning of a word. All of these prefixes make a word mean the **opposite**. Choose the correct prefix from those below to add to the words.

un-	dis-	il-	im-	non-	ir-	in-	mis-

1. _____ important
2. _____ understanding
3. _____ reversible
4. _____ mature
5. _____ fiction
6. _____ regular
7. _____ delible
8. _____ guided
9. _____ possible
10. _____ sense
11. _____ forgivable
12. _____ inform

B The following prefixes are **prefixes of time**. Match each to their meaning.

pre-	again
re-	in front of
post-	before
fore-	former
ex-	after

C Each row of words needs the same **prefix** from the list above to complete all the words. Write it in the first column. It must fit all words.

1. _____ -school -arrange -mature
2. _____ -ground -head -sight
3. _____ -girlfriend -army -port
4. _____ -date -war -mortem
5. _____ -play -place -write

D Number prefixes—highlight or circle the prefix which is the highest number in each row.

1.	tri-	bi-	nona-	oct-
2.	uni-	centi-	duo-	hexa-
3.	tetra-	deca-	quadr-	mono-
4.	kilo-	semi-	demi-	cent-
5.	hept-	quint-	hex-	tri-
6.	semi-	tri-	pent-	bi-

47

Homographs

A Choose the **homograph** which matches both definitions. Write it in the last column.

can	bank	present	chest
watch	bat	tear	minute

1.	look at AND a timepiece	
2.	place to store money AND side of a river	
3.	tiny AND a unit of time	
4.	big box AND torso	
5.	hit a ball AND a flying creature	
6.	a rip AND something you cry	
7.	gift AND right now in time	
8.	tin AND being able to	

B For each of these homographs, identify 2 **meanings**.

No.	Word	Meaning 1	Meaning 2
1	bear		
2	saw		
3	wind		
4	fair		
5	well		
6	wave		

C In each row identify the one word which is **NOT** a homograph. Highlight or circle it.

1.	sink	boat	ship
2.	wind	hail	snow
3.	ribbon	tie	bow
4.	wave	cornet	sea
5.	wrong	right	left
6.	play	game	fun
7.	hour	second	minute
8.	bark	branch	tree

Synonyms

A Choose the word that is closest in meaning, a synonym, to replace the word in bold.
All the words describe **feelings and emotions**.

thrilled	motivated	nervous	resentful	uncertain	optimistic

1. Jodi felt really **ANXIOUS** _____ about the forthcoming test.

2. The chess team were **EXHILERATED** _____ after their win.

3. Marcus was **DOUBTFUL** _____ about his team's chances.

4. Faiza felt **ANGRY** _____ when her brother sat in the front again.

5. The careers talk **INSPIRED** _____ Mimi to pursue medicine.

6. Sanuvi was always **POSITIVE** _____ about any new adventure.

B **Match the synonyms** by drawing lines or colour coding.

danger	occupation
simple	live
coronet	elevate
profession	crown
dwell	hazard
lift	easy

C Which of the words is **NOT a synonym** for the word in bold?

1.	small	devious	miniature	diminutive
2.	careful	alert	cautious	daring
3.	angry	infantile	infuriated	enraged
4.	house	habitat	dwelling	dormant
5.	cost	change	price	fee
6.	follow	stalk	detain	pursue
7.	calm	tranquil	inhale	placid
8.	large	vessel	immense	colossal

D List as many synonyms as you can for each of the words in bold. Use a thesaurus if you are unsure.

1. LOOK _____

2. SCARY _____

3. FAST _____

Antonyms

A Pair up the antonyms from the chart by writing them out below. Cross them out or highlight to eliminate them as you go to make it easier.

ancient	foe	fake	reckless	genuine	cautious
plain	innocent	elaborate	guilty	modern	ally

1. _____ and _____   2. _____ and _____

3. _____ and _____   4. _____ and _____

5. _____ and _____   6. _____ and _____

B Choose a word from the selection below to replace each word in capitals with one which means **the opposite**. You may need to change the article (a) to an.

methodical	cultivated	amateur	miserable
deliberate	modest	shallow	vacant

1. The garden was full of **WILD** _____ plants.

2. His preferred holiday home was **OCCUPIED** _____ .

3. Their referee decided the push was **ACCIDENTAL** _____ .

4. Rumi now played for a **PROFESSIONAL** _____ cricket team.

5. The office space was organised in a **RANDOM** _____ way.

6. Along by the bridge, the river was really **DEEP** _____ .

7. The sportsman was **PROUD** _____ about his achievements.

8. Whatever was happening, Ada was always **CHEERFUL** _____ .

C Choose the **antonym** for the underlined word. Select only one option.

1. **unnecessary**
   A) purchase   **B)** wanted   **C)** essential   **D)** chosen

2. **energetic**
   A) tiresome   **B)** sporty   **C)** inactive   **D)** active

3. **public**
   A) inside   **B)** people   **C)** last   **D)** private

4. **cluttered**
   A) tidy   **B)** cupboard   **C)** piled   **D)** messy

5. **fail**
   A) do   **B)** score   **C)** trophy   **D)** accomplish

6. **capture**
   A) imprison   **B)** release   **C)** win   **D)** punish

Word Combinations

A **Prepositional phrases** require particular prepositions to be used with particular words. Add these prepositions to the words in bold to complete these. Use each once only.

in	by	for	at	on

1. _____ **anticipation** of the party, she bought a new outfit.

2. Her mother was annoyed as she said that the children took her _____ **granted**.

3. They had to learn all their times tables _____ **heart**.

4. With traffic _____ **a standstill**, they knew it would be a long journey.

5. Families have less than two children _____ **average** in this country.

B Certain activities that we do require a specific verb – these are **verb collocations**. Complete the verb collocations below by putting them with the correct verb.

a difference	to sleep	a visit	online
a look	a compliment	the bed	astray
a decision	attention	responsibility	turns

go	take	make	pay

C Some well-known collocations involve adding an adverb and adjective together, such as 'utterly devastated' or 'hugely impressed'.
Choose the right adverb to complete these **adverb + adjective collocations**.

dimly	densely	tightly
highly	closely	pleasantly

1. Hong Kong is a _____ **populated** country.

2. Alex was _____ **surprised** by her aunt's present.

3. Granny's marmalade recipe was a _____ **guarded** secret.

4. Before posting, he ensured the packages were _____ **bound**.

5. From the ruined porch, they were led into a _____ **lit** passage.

6. Surprisingly, the cookie sale was _____ **profitable**.

Grammar Definitions

adjective

definition: ....

example: ....

adverb

definition: ....

example: ....

pronoun

definition: ....

example: ....

prefix

definition: ....

example: ....

suffix

definition: ....

example: ....

homograph

definition: ....

example: ....

synonym

definition: ....

example: ....

antonym

definition: ....

example: ....

collocation

definition: ....

example: ....

VOCABULARY
FOR
LITERATURE

Similes and Metaphors

Similes and metaphors are used to compare two things and are used frequently in literature, especially poetry.

Similes compare things by using 'like' or 'a'.   *The wind was like a beast.*

Metaphors simply describe one thing as if it is another.   *The wind was a beast.*

Similes and metaphors have qualities in common with the things with which they are compared. Here, we can imagine a wild, ferocious and uncontrollable wind.

A Identify whether the underlined phrase is a **simile** or **metaphor** by putting a S or M next to it.

1. He turned <u>white as a ghost</u>.   _____

2. Their neighbour had <u>a heart of gold</u>.   _____

3. The sun is <u>a golden disc</u>.   _____

4. He danced <u>like a lost spirit</u>.   _____

5. Her bedroom was <u>a rubbish tip</u>.   _____

6. <u>As cool as an evening breeze</u>, she walked in.   _____

B Sometimes a **metaphor** becomes so well known it becomes an **idiom**, an informal phrase which we use every day. Match the animal to complete each of these phrases.

Use colour coding or lines to link them and use each only once.

kangaroo	out
wolf	around
bull	in your pants
duck	court
ants	down your food
monkey	by the horns

C Equally, animals make good **similes** as well. Humans are often described like this to show that we share similar traits with that creature.

Complete the similes with the words from the chart.

snail	dog	bee	bird
mouse	owl	ox	eel

1. as busy as a(n) _____   2. as quiet as a(n) _____

3. as slippery as a(n) _____ 4. as wise as a(n) _____

5. as slow as a(n) _____   6. as strong as a(n) _____

7. as free as a(n) _____   8. as sick as a(n) _____

Personification

Personification is describing an inanimate object or an animal as if they are a 'person'.
The wind whispered in the trees.
The word 'whispered' is a verb and 'whispering' is something people do, not trees.
It is used to suggest the quiet sound made.
Often, personification uses verbs like this, but it can also be created with nouns or adjectives.

A Choose a **verb** to personify each of these objects and to complete the sentences.
Only use each one once.

winked	controlled	danced	refused	stroked	groaned

1. The chimney _____ under the force of the wind.

2. As I lay there, the grasses gently _____ my face.

3. The sun _____ at me in a knowing way and I smiled back.

4. Unfortunately, although I was late, the car _____ to budge.

5. With each surge, the waves _____ to their own rhythm.

6. The computer _____ me – I was no longer responsible.

B Choose a **noun** to personify each object and to complete the sentences.

limb	coat	eyes	mouth	heart	mind

1. In the _____ of the forest lurked a terrible secret.

2. The tree stretched one long _____ towards me.

3. Unfortunately, my skateboard seemed to have a _____ of its own.

4. Even the house shuddered and drew its _____ tightly around it.

5. The castle stared down at me with its square, yellowy _____.

6. In the _____ of the cave, I hesitated before entering.

C Underline or highlight the **adjective** which is personifying an object in each sentence.
Be careful as there may be other adjectives in the sentence.

1. The comforting fireplace was ablaze on that moonlit night.

2. With each passing second, the determined wind increased in strength.

3. Swinging idly, the lazy door opened and closed with each gust.

4. To her relief, the thoughtful clock struck six times to tell her the time.

5. A spiteful chill was felt by the ill-dressed children.

6. The stubborn games console would not work in spite of her furious protests.

Sound Words

The sounds of words are often used by writers to create particular moods or to emphasise words which sound similar.

Alliteration – this is repetition of the first letter of words next to or near each other.
Sibilance – this is repetition of the 's' sound – it does not need to be at the beginning.
Assonance – this is repetition of vowel sounds – a, e, i, o, u.

A Identify the sound devices being used in these sentences. One uses 2 devices.
Choose from **alliteration, sibilance** and **assonance.**

1. Green grass grew abundantly. _____

2. A bitter and chill wind pierced them. _____

3. Later, a lovely lullaby lured her to sleep. _____

4. Essential support surrounded them. _____

5. The bark was breaking on the battling waves. _____

6. A sinister sense of something staring gripped her. _____

B Tongue twisters use **alliteration**, challenging us to say them aloud. Add adjectives and verbs to these to create tongue twisters. The first is done.
Concentrate on the sound you create.

Number	Adjective	Noun	Verb (past)
One	*orange*	*orangutan*	*observed*
Two		turtles	
Four		foxes	
Six		seahorses	
Nine		newts	
Ten		terriers	

C Add words to this **cloze passage** to make it make sense. All of the words you add should make alliterative phrases so use this to help you.

green	refreshing	scorching	lonely
broken	delicious	aching	many

Gerri ambled along the **1.** _____ lane, pushing her **2.** _____ bicycle. She was still

3. _____ miles from her home and the **4.** _____ sky created an unbearable heat.

Thinking of the **5.** _____ river she had left behind, Gerri longed to collapse on the

6. _____ grass by the side of the road. However, her **7.** _____ appetite spurred

her on with the thought of the **8.** _____ dinner which was waiting for her.

Onomatopoeia

Onomatopoeia is a word which sounds like its meaning. There are many of them in the English language and writers use them to emphasise the meaning of these words. It means we can actually hear the sound being made.
Common examples include: **bang, whizz, thud, whirr**.

A Highlight or circle the word in each line which **sounds like its meaning**.

1. The sputter of the engine was the final proof that the car was finished.

2. The evening was punctuated by the murmuring of crickets in the distant field.

3. Finally, he blurted out the truth: he had finished the chocolate cake.

4. No one dared whisper in Mr Leech's class as his anger was legendary.

5. Although inwardly retching, Greta knew she had to eat her grandfather's stew.

6. With his final push, the cream squirted hopelessly over the floor.

7. Above them, the loud music blared from his brother's loudspeakers.

8. Delightedly, the children crunched their way through the new-fallen snow.

B Match the animals and objects up with the sounds they make. Use colour coding or lines to link them.

cat	pop
owl	zoom
bacon	hum
lion	smash
tap	sizzle
glass	roar
balloon	purr
bees	hoot
rocket	drip

C Writers choose sound words carefully to create different moods. Replace the words in bold with alternative sound words to **create a different mood**. Use each one only once.

thud	howling	crunch	babble	gasping	grating

Outside, in the night, she could hear the **humming 1.** _____ of animals and the

soothing 2. _____ sound of nearby traffic. There was also the low **whisper**

3. _____ of nearby voices and the **pad 4.** _____ of footsteps on the ground.

This was followed by a **tap 5.** _____ on the door and the unmistakable sound of

someone **breathing 6.** _____ .

Genre

A **genre** is a type of story. Genres include fantasy, adventure, horror, comedy and sci-fi. Writers use particular words to suggest which type of story they are writing as there are particular characters, settings and plots for each genre.

A Sort these words in the chart into the correct genre classification.

bombsite	inter-planetary	deep space	quest	front line
elves	evacuee	AI	military	midnight
clone	spirit	graveyard	creature	galactic
alien	sword	bunker	haunted house	king

fantasy	ghost	sci-fi	war

B Genres often rely on **opposites** or **antitheses**. These can be characters or values or ideas. Match up these antitheses by colour coding or drawing lines.

knowledge	revenge
love	light
good	hate
forgiveness	wealth
hero	cowardice
bravery	ignorance
dark	villain
poverty	evil

C Match the term to the definition.

ballad	biography	dystopian	haiku	novella	parable

1. an account of someone's life _____

2. a short, Japanese poem _____

3. a short tale with a moral _____

4. a poem that tells a story _____

5. a short novel _____

6. a story set in a dreadful future _____

Writing about Fiction

When we write about fiction, we are often asked to give our opinion about mood and atmosphere. It is useful to have a wide vocabulary when we do this.

A Identify the **2 synonyms** you could use to describe **mood** in the same way as the word in bold. Circle or highlight the ones closest in meaning.

1.	**dark**	moon	shaded	gloomy	cold
2.	**happy**	lovely	jubilant	welcome	upbeat
3.	**sad**	melancholy	cuddly	depressing	frightening
4.	**funny**	stupid	light-hearted	tense	comical
5.	**scary**	wild	gracious	haunting	fearful

B Replace the bold 'thought' word or phrase in these sentences with the best, alternative. Use each one only once and think carefully about which fits best.

reflected	studied	considered	examined	meditated	investigated

1. I **thought** _____ on the meaning of life.

2. He **thought about** _____ all of his revision books.

3. They **thought about** _____ the crime.

4. After, when she **thought** _____, she realised she was wrong.

5. I **thought about** _____ all my options and decided to go.

6. The squad **thought about** _____ the evidence carefully.

C Writers appeal to all the **senses** to create mood. Find 2 words or phrases in this passage for each sense.

A dim light was flickering in the distance as he groped his way through the prickly brambles and stinging nettles. Breathing heavily, he could almost taste the remnants of a damp, autumn bonfire. The burning smell hung in the air, half-choking, filling the dead woodland with a mist-like smoke. Through the spiky branches, the outline of a ruined cottage was becoming visible. There was a low hum, like something electrical being used and a tinny radio sound from the same direction. His feet sunk into the damp moss and his nostrils caught the whiff of decay.

sight	**smell**	**touch**	**sound**

Vocabulary for Literature Definitions

<u>simile</u>

definition: ....

example: ....

<u>metaphor</u>

definition: ....

example: ....

<u>idiom</u>

definition: ....

example: ....

<u>personification</u>

definition: ....

example: ....

<u>alliteration</u>

definition: ....

example: ....

<u>sibilance</u>

definition: ....

example: ....

<u>assonance</u>

definition: ....

example: ....

<u>onomatopoeia</u>

definition: ....

example: ....

<u>genre</u>

definition: ....

example: ....

<u>antithesis</u>

definition: ....

example: ....

VOCABULARY MEANING AND CONTEXT

Comprehension

A Read the passage and then identify the word closest in meaning to the bold word *as it is used in this context*. Circle or highlight the word.

> Dogs are **vastly** superior to cats in so many ways that it is almost pointless to make this statement. They form **genuine** attachments and actually care when you are upset, whereas cats only **operate** on their own terms. If they want food, a door opening or **emotional** support, they will **demand** it. However, do not expect them to offer comfort when you need it. That **sly** look is judging and **assessing** you **constantly** and a cat will never completely let down its guard.

1.	**vastly**	always	mainly	hugely
2.	**genuine**	deep	real	long
3.	**operate**	work	play	eat
4.	**emotional**	thought	inner	substantial
5.	**demand**	order	require	want
6.	**sly**	evil	dark	cunning
7.	**assessing**	considering	counting	dismissing
8.	**constantly**	tirelessly	continuously	desperately

B Read the passage and then identify the word closest in meaning to the bold word *as it is used in this context*. Circle or highlight the word.

> Ellie had always had a special **flair** for football. At the age of three, she had **irritated** her older brother by taking his ball at every opportunity. Now, she rang rings around any team and left her **opponents** standing, **gazing** at her with disbelief. Today though was a **crucial** day for her as she was going to be doing trials for a club in the top **league**. For someone who was always **serene**, her nerves were **alarming** that morning.

1.	**flair**	position	talent	desire
2.	**irritated**	annoyed	inspired	overtook
3.	**opponents**	enemies	teammates	rivals
4.	**gazing**	shouting	staring	darting
5.	**crucial**	frightening	spectacular	important
6.	**league**	division	county	bracket
7.	**serene**	quiet	calm	moody
8.	**alarming**	cold	dark	disturbing

Root Words

A Identify the **root words** in each of these words. Remember to remove any prefixes and suffixes. These are 'free' root words which make sense on their own.

1. reformation _____
2. enactment _____
3. unmanageable _____
4. dishonesty _____
5. hopefully _____
6. unluckily _____
7. preheated _____
8. disconnection _____

B Make **2 new words** from the free root word, using a **prefix** and then a **suffix**. You may have to change the ending for the suffix. Example: *loud* becomes 'aloud' and 'loudness'.

root word	with a prefix	with a suffix
1. happy		
2. plant		
3. correct		
4. place		
5. do		
6. like		
7. clear		
8. view		

C Some root words are 'bound' which means they need other parts to make a word. However, they have a clear meaning of their own.

Match these Greek and Latin **'bound' root words** with their meanings. Colour code or draw lines to link them.

multi-	heat
astro-	world
bio-	measure
micro-	race
ethno	life
therm-	star
cosmo-	many
meter-	small

Cloze

A **cloze passage** has words missing and you have to decide which words should be used to complete the passage. Many 11 plus tests include these tasks.
A selection of words is given and this tests your reading skills and ability to work out the best vocabulary to fit in the context of a sentence.

A This is a cloze passage about **school**. Read it carefully to help you work out which words to use to complete the passage. Each word can only be used once.

knowledge	primary	qualities	subjects
activities	socialising	education	secondary

School is the place we all go for our **1.** _____ and it is generally divided into

2. _____ for younger children up to eleven and then **3.** _____ school from

then on until we leave. Schools provide us with all kinds of **4.** _____ and that is split

up into many different **5.** _____ such as science and geography. However, we develop

other **6.** _____ as well like the skill of **7.** _____ and teamwork. School can also

introduce us to a range of **8.** _____ such as sports, dance, art and music.

B This is a cloze passage about **computer games**. Read it carefully to help you work out which words to use to complete the passage. Each word can only be used once.

code	levels	motivated	thought	online
setting	feedback	challenge	screen	score

Many children love playing computer games and a lot of **1.** _____ goes into making them.

Designers use computer **2.** _____ to create each possible action in a game and place the

characters in a **3.** _____ where there are many choices and decisions you can make.

They use different **4.** _____ which get more difficult as you progress through them.

These help to keep us **5.** _____ as we want to get higher. We also get continuous

6. _____ on our performance with a total or **7.** _____ that we see in the corner

of the **8.** _____. Many games also allow us to play **9.** _____ with our friends to

make it more competitive and more of a **10.** _____.

C In each row, circle or highlight the **odd word out** which does not fit the topic.

1.	ball	racquet	shuttlecock	badminton
2.	theatre	play	stage	camera
3.	pen	felt tip	rubber	pencil
4.	cod	crab	lobster	prawn

Word Relationships

A Sort these **family** members into male, female or not stated (could be either).

uncle	in-law	grandfather	fiancé
mother	nephew	wife	niece
grandchild	nanny	cousin	son

male	**female**	**not stated**

B All of these **professions** end in '-er', '-or' or '-ian'. Add the correct ending to each.

1. profess _____

2. teach _____

3. doct _____

4. music _____

5. photograph _____

6. librar _____

7. act _____

8. veterinar _____

C Match these '**part**' to '**whole**' words to identify what is part of what.
Only use each word once.

fin	shoe
rind	seasons
chapter	fish
leg	lemon
sole	book
spring	table

Now, state what the 'whole' is from these parts.

1. stem, root, bud _____

2. knuckle, digit, thumb _____

3. engine, boot, dashboard _____

4. leg, arm, cushion _____

5. crust, slice, yeast _____

6. dungeon, tower, rampart _____

Shuffle

A In a **shuffled sentence** you need to put the sentence in the right order and then identify the extra word. The extra word is not needed in the sentence. These are all about 'baddies'.

1. **hunt eyepatches wear ship treasure pirates and.**

    Sentence: _____

    Extra word: _____

2. **cloak has teeth huge and blood black a Dracula.**

    Sentence: _____

    Extra word: _____

3. **plotted little eat wolf to house pigs three the.**

    Sentence: _____

    Extra word: _____

4. **labryrinth in lived mountain deep a Minotaur the.**

    Sentence: _____

    Extra word: _____

5. **wand a Voldemort magician snakes to dangerous and was talked Lord.**

    Sentence: _____

    Extra word: _____

6. **throw little to school loved Trunchbull children.**

    Sentence: _____

    Extra word: _____

B All of these **shuffled words** name **colours**. Can you unscramble them from the clues?

1.	LOVETI	light shade of purple	_____
2.	ZEROBN	a dull gold colour	_____
3.	YONBE	dark black	_____
4.	LAHZE	reddish brown, tree	_____
5.	MAOLSN	pinkish orange	_____
6.	RNYUUDGB	dark purplish red	_____
7.	LATE	bluish green shade	_____
8.	RIYOV	bleached white	_____

Degrees of Meaning

Our choice of vocabulary depends on the meanings we want to create. One of those is **'degrees'** – how large or small something is; how weak or strong an emotion is; how forceful something is; how dark or light or cold or hot something is.

Our choice of vocabulary therefore depends on context as words mean slightly different things, even if they are synonyms.

A **Comparatives and superlatives** show the degree of something, with 'more' or an ending used for comparatives and 'most' or a suffix used for superlatives.

Complete this **comparatives and superlatives** chart. You may need to use 'more' and 'most' for some words.

both	comparative	superlative
dirty	*dirtier*	*dirtiest*
1. strange		
2. beautiful		
3. many		
4. thin		
5. rare		
6. scary		
7. handsome		
8. big		

B We need to select our **synonyms** carefully as they show different degrees of the same thing. Here, you should choose the word which is **'greatest' or most extreme** version of the word in bold. Circle or highlight the word.

1.	big	large	gigantic	great
2.	hot	warm	baking	flushed
3.	tired	exhausted	drooping	fatigued
4.	hurt	injured	sore	disfigured
5.	angry	enraged	cross	fuming
6.	confused	puzzled	bewildered	unsure
7.	disgusted	repulsed	displeased	fed up
8.	sorry	regretful	apologetic	remorseful

Vocabulary, Meaning and Context Tasks

A Ring or highlight the 6 words which could be used to describe someone's **facial expression**. They must all be adjectives.

thoughtful	perfectly	desperation	mischievous
invitation	baffled	crestfallen	total
ashamed	cobbled	fried	enraged

B The instructions for doing a test are in the **wrong order**. Label them 1 – 5 to show the correct order.

1. Open the paper.   _____

2. Check your work carefully and correct any errors.   _____

3. Read the questions very carefully.   _____

4. Write your name on the front of the paper.   _____

5. Put your pen down when told to finish.   _____

6. Attempt all the questions.   _____

C All of these words are **synonyms**. You need to choose the **best fit** for each of the sentences. Read them carefully and each should only be used once.

disturbed	unsettled
tormented	bothered

1. Indi could not be _____ to make her bed.

2. After three hours, they were completely _____ by the drilling.

3. He had _____ his father at work twice already today.

4. With the high temperatures, they all had an _____ night's sleep.

CREATIVE VOCABULARY

Levels of Formality

Whenever we write, we need to be aware of context – who will be reading it, where it will be seen, its purpose. Most of the time writing will be formal but sometimes, for pieces like poetry, speech and scripts, we may use informal language.

A For **friends and family**, we often use **informal language.** What is the formal version of each of these words?

1. cuz _____

2. nan _____

3. bro _____

4. kid _____

5. sis _____

6. mum _____

B Greetings and goodbyes are frequently informal as they are often shared by people close to each other. From these rows, pick the **most formal version** of what is said by highlighting or circling it.

1.	hey	hi	howdy	hello
2.	How's it going?	What's up?	How are you?	How's life?
3.	so long	goodbye	catch you later	laters
4.	soz	my apologies	sorry	sorry about that
5.	thank you	cheers	ta	thanks
6.	cool	brill	fab	fantastic

C Contractions are used frequently in informal language. Write out the full version of each of these contractions.

1. they've _____

2. we'd _____

3. I'll _____

4. won't _____

5. can't _____

6. you'll _____

D **Abbreviations** are also commonly used in informal language. Write these ones out in full.

1. m8 _____

2. asap _____

3. rd. _____

4. no. _____

5. btw _____

6. lol _____

7. ppl _____

8. gtg _____

Speech

A There are many different words we can use instead of 'said'. However, their meanings are different. Sort these 'said' words into categories based on the impression they create of a character.

bawled	barked	joked	hissed
gaped	chuckled	screeched	gasped
exclaimed	cried	moaned	jested

angry	surprised	sad	upbeat

B In speech we use a lot of idioms or sayings. These are unique to each language. Complete these English idioms by matching them up with colour coding or lines. These are all used to describe people.

as nutty as	of gold
as old as	in a sweet shop
sleeps	in the neck
babe	of all trades
a heart	in the woods
like a kid	a fruitcake
jack	time
a real pain	like a baby

C Identify the word nearest in meaning to the one in bold. These are the closest **synonyms**.

1.	**boasted**	bragged	blurted	barked
2.	**announced**	told	examined	proclaimed
3.	**soothed**	promised	reassured	pledged
4.	**whimpered**	shouted	whispered	whined
5.	**scolded**	reprimanded	reviewed	hesitated
6.	**rejected**	trembled	refused	wondered
7.	**assessed**	asked	elevated	evaluated
8.	**enquired**	frowned	queried	blamed

71

Linking Ideas

When we write, it is really important to link our ideas. Linking within paragraphs is called cohesion and linking between paragraphs is coherence. We use words and phrases which 'connect' our writing.

A Identify how we use each of these **cohesive words and phrases**. Some are used to 'add' to an idea, some to put ideas in 'order' and some to show difference.

Put them in the correct categories.

also	but	additionally
however	firstly	unlike this
lastly	too	secondly

adding	ordering	difference

B When we write, we often want to show a shift in **time.** There are a range of words which we use for this. Match up the words with their synonyms.

tomorrow	earlier
now	following
yesterday	at the same time
sooner	the day after
meanwhile	at present
next	the day before

C Complete the **cloze passage** by using each **conjunction** once only.

whenever	if	because	so	until

1. _____ the summer holidays start, the Tooth Fairy has a busy time. There are many more lost teeth at that time **2.** _____ children suddenly start being a lot more active. **3.** _____ all the children suddenly start visiting parks and jumping around on beaches, the chance of bumps and bangs goes up immensely. This means the Tooth Fairy has to pay out handfuls of shiny coins **4.** _____ she is broke **5.** _____ they go back to school.

Creating Characters

A One of the key aspects of a character is their personality type. This task requires you to find a synonym which shows better use of vocabulary.

Select a **synonym** for the word in bold to describe the same personality type. Choose the word *closest in meaning*.

1.	**organised**	logical	list	confident
2.	**loud**	amusing	outspoken	hysterical
3.	**forgetful**	impolite	adventurous	absent-minded
4.	**crazy**	eccentric	testing	adorable
5.	**greedy**	horrible	self-centred	hungry
6.	**intelligent**	connected	kind	astute
7.	**thoughtful**	thinking	considerate	deliberate
8.	**loyal**	devoted	reasonable	alert

B We also use vocabulary to describe physical features. Match up the **adjective** (descriptive word) with the body part it could best describe.

chiselled	eyes
oval	gait
tangled	nose
hazel	hair
clumsy	cheekbones
upturned	face

C Select an **antonym** (word with opposite meaning) to replace each word in bold to completely alter the meaning of these character descriptions.

stubby	unruly	withdrawn	sleek	obese	sullen	rosy	full

1. Freya had a **pasty** _____ complexion.

2. What you noticed first was the man's **trimmed** _____ beard.

3. Kaia's **thin** _____ lips were embellished with ruby lipstick.

4. Deena noted the man's **dull,** _____ long hair.

5. By the pier, the **lean** _____ teenager stared into the sea.

6. With **elegant** _____ hands, she picked up the child.

7. Neo had always been a **lively** _____ baby.

8. With her **sunny** _____ disposition, Andi stood out.

Settings with Attitude

Describing a setting is more than just telling your readers where something can happen. With the right vocabulary, a setting can create mood and expectation, reveal genre and even reflect a character's personality.

A Select the words which would *best* help create the moods in bold. It could be a synonym or just a detail which would fit the **mood.**

Highlight or circle one of the three options.

1.	**haunting**	stage	cobweb	handle
2.	**peaceful**	meadow	field	land
3.	**lonely**	garden	path	empty
4.	**tense**	derelict	crisp	building
5.	**cold**	weather	glacial	expression
6.	**celebratory**	land	endure	bunting

B When creating a setting, vocabulary can have negative or positive associations, while some words are neutral. Neutral words rely on context for their associations.

Classify these words according to **positive, negative and neutral**.

damp	dank	green	liberating	calm
pleasant	main	familiar	short	faint
near	warm	jagged	miserable	ideal

positive	negative	neutral

C Match up the objects to the genre where you would find them. Draw lines or colour code.

war	horse, saloon, arrow
sport	aristocrat, past, manor
western	charm, villain, treasure
biography	shell, armoury, troop
historical	date, family, achievement
fantasy	pitch, champion, award

Attitude and Tone

The words we use as writers reveal our attitude towards the topic and our readers. These create the tone of our writing. We describe the tone using adjectives like angry, sad, upbeat, argumentative and thoughtful.

A Pair up the **antonyms** to show opposite tones. Use lines or colour coding.

joyous	serious
relaxed	nightmarish
forgiving	directionless
humorous	vengeful
dream-like	tense
purposeful	heartbroken

B Identify the tone of these sentences by selecting one of the **tone words**. Only use each once.

fearful	sarcastic	passionate
depressed	furious	comforting

1. Chocolate and sleep are truly two of life's wonders. _____

2. As the steps approached, she trembled uncontrollably. _____

3. Do not worry as I will help you find your teddy. _____

4. The lonely wind moaned and wept the whole night. _____

5. Look at the 'genius' who can't even spell the word. _____

6. If I do not hear back today, I will speak to your boss. _____

C Circle or highlight the word which is **closest in meaning** to the word in bold. It will be a which shows the same attitude.

1.	**disappointed**	disgraced	deliberate	upset
2.	**excited**	great	thrilled	grave
3.	**proud**	arrogant	harsh	succeed
4.	**hopeful**	wild	optimistic	wary
5.	**romantic**	message	close	loving
6.	**kind**	thoughtful	chosen	peaceful
7.	**crazy**	creepy	hateful	zany
8.	**daring**	gloomy	bold	critical

Creative Vocabulary Definitions

contraction

definition: ....

example: ....

formal language

definition: ....

example: ....

informal language

definition: ....

example: ....

abbreviation

definition: ....

example: ....

cohesion

definition: ....

example: ....

coherence

definition: ....

example: ....

tone

definition: ....

example: ....

mood

definition: ....

example: ....

VOCABULARY
GAMES

Adding and Taking Letters

A Add 1 letter to these words to create a new word. Write out the new word and letter.

1. BEND   Add letter: _____ to make new word: _____

2. SORE   Add letter: _____ to make new word: _____

3. SAND   Add letter: _____ to make new word: _____

4. TEAM   Add letter: _____ to make new word: _____

5. DARE   Add letter: _____ to make new word: _____

6. ROAD   Add letter: _____ to make new word: _____

7. BEAK   Add letter: _____ to make new word: _____

8. SPOT   Add letter: _____ to make new word: _____

B Swap the letter indicated for another one to make a new word. If we started with 'lake', we could change the 'k' to make 'lame' or 'late' for instance.

1. RARE   Swap the second 'R'.   New word: _____

2. HELP   Swap the 'L'.   New word: _____

3. SNOW   Swap the 'N'.   New word: _____

4. VERY   Swap the 'E'.   New word: _____

5. GRAB   Swap the 'G'.   New word: _____

6. VASE   Swap the 'E'.   New word: _____

7. SOLD   Swap the 'D'.   New word: _____

8. BATS   Swap the 'S'.   New word: _____

C Move a letter from the first to the second word to make 2 new words. Write out the new words. Do not alter the order of the letters.

1. FOUND   HARD   makes _____ and _____.

2. THORN   HEART   makes _____ and _____.

3. TABLE   LESS   makes _____ and _____.

4. CHART   INSET   makes _____ and _____.

5. CLAMP   ABLE   makes _____ and _____.

6. SIFTS   RILE   makes _____ and _____.

Hidden Words

A Find the **3-letter word** hidden in this word. The letters will not change order. There may be more than one possible answer.

1. CREATED   Hidden word/s: _____

2. TERRIBLE   Hidden word/s: _____

3. DESTINATION   Hidden word/s: _____

4. INNOVATOR   Hidden word/s: _____

5. IRRELEVANT   Hidden word/s: _____

6. INDEPENDENT   Hidden word/s: _____

7. PORRIDGE   Hidden word/s: _____

8. MEANDER   Hidden word/s: _____

B Now, find the **4-letter words** between these pairs of words and write them out. They may use 2 letters from each word or 1 and 3 letters from the 2 words.

1. **soda taste**   4-letter word: _____

2. **talented artist** 4-letter word: _____

3. **human years**   4-letter word: _____

4. **great earnings**   4-letter word: _____

5. **your germs**   4-letter word: _____

6. **plump rowers**   4-letter word: _____

7. **vivid eagles**   4-letter word: _____

8. **robe stunner**   4-letter word: _____

C These hidden words are **anagrams**. You can rearrange the letters to make another word. These are very common in crosswords. There may be more than one answer.

1. **SHOE** can be rearranged to make   _____.

2. **TIRE** can be rearranged to make   _____.

3. **EATS** can be rearranged to make   _____.

4. **SNOW** can be rearranged to make   _____.

5. **NOSE** can be rearranged to make   _____.

6. **FOWL** can be rearranged to make   _____.

7. **BRAG** can be rearranged to make   _____.

8. **PETS** can be rearranged to make   _____.

79

Relationships

A Put these words into the right **family categories**.

rolling pin	broccoli	tongs	pasty
paella	spoon	vinegar	grater
basil	garlic	trifle	pepper
sieve	stew	spatula	flour

ingredients	utensils	recipes

B Match these **workers** to **a tool** they might use by colour coding or drawing lines.

surgeon	saucepan
mechanic	buoy
seamstress	rake
chef	truncheon
barrister	spanner
police officer	scalpel
gardener	wig
lifeguard	needle

C Which word is the **odd one out** in each row? The others are all related by a topic. Circle or highlight the 'odd' word.

1.	coconut	watermelon	parsnip	mango
2.	lunch	supper	tea	dinner
3.	spend	save	buy	purchase
4.	cot	scooter	dummy	nappy
5.	apartment	flat	bedsit	bungalow
6.	cougar	courage	courageous	encourage

Vocabulary Games – Missing in Action

A Select the words to complete this **cloze passage** about flags of the world.

shapes	patriotic	sky	colour
cross	country	values	century

Every **1.** _____ in the world will have its own flag which is used as a

2. _____ symbol telling you about that place and some of its ideas and

3. _____ . There are common symbols like those to do with the **4.** _____

such as the moon, sun or stars. Other flags have particular **5.** _____ like

circles or squares. A common feature is the distinctive **6.** _____ combinations

with primary colours being the most popular. The oldest flag in the world is the one

from Denmark which was first used in the 13th **7.** _____ which has a white

8. _____ on a red background.

B Identify the **missing 3-letter words** which will complete all of the words in capitals.
They must be real words and then you will have the correct spelling.

1. On **AVE**_____**E**, we eat 35 tons of food in our lives.

2. Lennie felt **AWK**_____**D** meeting new people.

3. The spaniel was a lovely **COM**_____**ION** for his nan.

4. It was so **T**_____**QUIL** and calm in the beautiful garden.

5. Lily was **S**_____**BORN** and she refused to listen.

6. **L**_____**LINESS** is a big problem for many old people.

7. The police **DESC**_____**TION** matched the man exactly.

8. The **COM**_____**ATION** of cheese and pickle was perfect.

C Fill in the missing letters to complete the **antonyms**.

1. **FAMOUS**   UN__NO__N.

2. **BEGINNING**   CO__C__US__ON.

3. **PROFESSIONAL**   A__AT__UR.

4. **EDUCATED**   I__NO__ANT.

5. **GUILTY**   __NNO__ENT.

6. **DEMAND**   S__PP__Y.

7. **ALLOW**   F__R__ID.

8. **COMBINE**   SE__AR__TE.

Combining Words

A Pair the words to make 8 **compound words**. Each word can only be used once. Highlight or cross them out after you have used them.

take	stop	off	sweet
coach	snow	shell	watch
egg	heart	stand	tail
by	pony	drift	stage

1. _____

2. _____

3. _____

4. _____

5. _____

6. _____

7. _____

8. _____

B Choose a letter which can **end one word** and **start the next**. One letter must complete both words.

1. cres ___ race

2. bruis ___ lect

3. hast ___ ield

4. peri ___ atter

5. decei ___ yrant

6. oat ___ umble

7. inhabi ___ orment

8. weir ___ espise

C Add the correct suffix to these words to turn them into adverbs.
You may need to lose or change a letter. Each suffix can be used more than once.

-ally
-ly
-ily

1. **luck**   Adverb: _____

2. **kind**   Adverb: _____

3. **angry**   Adverb: _____

4. **basic**   Adverb: _____

5. **magic**   Adverb: _____

6. **tidy**   Adverb: _____

7. **scientific** Adverb: _____

8. **faithful**   Adverb: _____

Playing with Words

A Change each word into another by changing only 1 letter at a time. See how quickly you can do it with a timer or competing with a friend.

Example: **kind to mean**: *kind, mind, mend, mead, mean.*

1. **STOP** to **FLEW**

   STOP _____

   _____

2. **FAST** to **SLOW**

   FAST _____

   _____

3. **GOLD** to **DUST**

   GOLD _____

   _____

B How many words can you make out of **ACCIDENTALLY**? Only use each letter as often as it appears. The letters can be in any order. Take each consonant in turn to help you make more words, such as words beginning with 'T'. Time yourself or compete with a friend.

ACCIDENTALLY

_____

_____

_____

_____

_____

_____

_____

_____

C Put these words in **alphabetical order** and work out which is last.

1. happy, hug, huge, hungry   Last word: _____

2. angry, anger, apple, approach   Last word: _____

3. rare, rash, rabbit, rail   Last word: _____

4. mice, meal, nest, mope   Last word: _____

5. queen, quick quaint, quail   Last word: _____

6. fond, feign, found, forest   Last word: _____

83

ANSWERS

Animals (p. 6-7)

A cheetah and cub, horse and foal, deer and fawn, falcon and chick, swan and cygnet, goat and kid

B **reptiles** – lizard, crocodile, alligator, snake, tortoise
mammals – panda, wolf, whale
birds – flamingo, crow, starling, owl, ostrich
fish – shark, octopus, mackerel
amphibians – frog, newt, salamander, toad

C
1. amphibians
2. fish
3. mammals
4. reptiles
5. birds

D snort – antelope, growl – bear, screech – bat, bleat – goat, caw – crow, honk – goose

E
1. flamingoes; add '-es'
2. wolves; change 'f' to 'v' and add '-es'
3. hippopotami; change 'us' to '-i'
4. the plural is the same as the singular
5. oxen
6. mice
7. geese
8. lice

F pride – lions, army – ants, pod – dolphins, train – camels herd – cows, pack – wolves

Trees, Plants and Flowers (p. 8-9)

A holly bush – berry
cherry tree – blossom
palm tree – coconut
oak tree – acorn
horse chestnut tree – conker
pine tree – needle

B
1. cactus and holly
2. tangerine and lemon
3. mushroom and toadstool
4. carnation and daffodil
5. oak and elm
6. bamboo
7. mistletoe

C
1. climates
2. ingredients
3. sunlight (or water)
4. water (or sunlight)
5. roots
6. sprout
7. stem
8. leaves
9. pollinate
10. cycle

D These can be in any order.
1. **palm** – type of tree; hand; 'palm off' – dismiss someone
2. **pine** – type of tree; mourn or weep for someone gone
3. **branch** – tree branch; another part of an organisation / business

E
1. thorn
2. stalk
3. cultivate
4. bush
5. produce
6. seed
7. vine
8. sprig

F
1. plant – put in the ground
2. germinate – begin to grow
3. sprout – put out shoots
4. blossom – produce flowers
5. die – lose life
6. seed – seed produced for next growth

Weather (p.10-11)

A **thaw** (snow, ice) and **rainbow** (rain, sun) can fit into 2 groups
snow – flake, sleet, slush, flurry
wind – gale, cyclone, tornado,
rain – flood, thunder, lightning
sun – drought, heatwave
ice – frost, icicle

B
1. hot, hotter, hottest
2. chilly, chillier, chilliest
3. refreshing, more refreshing, most refreshing
4. damp, damper, dampest
5. clear, clearer, clearest
6. strong, stronger, strongest

C
1. mist
2. hurricane
3. tempest
4. blazing
5. breezy
6. avalanche

D
1. weather
2. temperature
3. degrees
4. Fahrenheit (or Celsius)
5. Celsius (or Fahrenheit)
6. freezing
7. wind
8. forecast
9. rain (or sunshine)
10. sunshine (or rain)

E thunderstorm, snowflake, sunbathe, sunburn, rainbow, thunderbolt, hailstorm, snowstorm, sunburn, raincloud, raihstorm

Words within Words (p. 12)

A Meteorological - suggestions:

large, merge, trace, greet, actor, image, agree, cello, green, glare, metal, grill

B Amphibians - suggestions:

pains, mains, basin, lambs, banish, mine, ship, mash, maps, spin, shin, mini, snip

Body Matters (p. 14-15)

A chest – torso, leg – limb, chin – jaw, brain – mind, spine – back

B ear – smell, lobe, drum, canal
nose – nostril, smell, nasal cavity, septum, bridge
mouth – lips, taste, tongue, gum, teeth, tonsils
eye – brow, pupil, sight, lens, lid, iris

C
1. murmur
2. yell
3. weep
4. disagree
5. saunter
6. parade
7. hobble
8. roam

D
1. see, hear
2. leg, arm
3. pump, digest
4. metre, kilo
5. hand, foot
6. thirst, hunger

E
1. PIT
2. RAT
3. LET
4. TIN
5. ACT
6. LOG

F
1. vein and artery
2. tibia and femur
3. liver and lung
4. wrist and digit
5. fever and swelling
6. molar and canine

Dressing Up (p. 16-17)

A
1. **suit** – matching items of clothing; to complement or go well with something
2. **coat** – outer garment; to spread over something
3. **dress** – garment; to dress someone or something

B **top** – turtleneck, blouse, hoodie, poncho, anorak
bottom – sarong, kilt, tutu, trunks, jodhpurs
head – balaclava, sombrero, visor
feet – moccasin, slipper, mule

C
1. She was freezing in spite of her

woolly hat and scarf. (snow)

2. They bought new outfits to wear to the school dance. (rules)

3. Kaftans can be made of wool, silk or cotton. (design)

4. Traditionally, many brides choose to have long veils. (ceremony)

D 1. gloves and scarf
(others are hats)

2. umbrella and gown
(others are coats)

3. sock and slipper
(others are shoes to be worn outside)

4. trunk and trolley
(others are bags to carry)

5. earring and ring
(others are worn on wrist)

6. show and carry
(others are synonyms to do with wearing)

E tracksuit, raincoat, sunglasses, necktie, headscarf, nightgown

F decoration, embellishment, adornment

Sport (p. 18-19)

A 1. bat, racquet

2. court, exorcise

3. goal, point

4. wait, queue

5. swimming, football

6. club, stick

B 1. to prepare for something; transport

2. active and well; to 'fit' in a space

3. to row a boat; argument

4. to take a recording; highest achievement in something; music EP

5. piece of equipment; to take your turn batting

6. to take part; theatre performance; perform a role

C 1. HER (archery)

2. LET (athletics)

3. TON (badminton)

4. RAT (karate)

5. NOW (snowboarding)

6. HUT (parachuting)

D 1. participate

2. physical

3. exercise

4. impact

5. organs

6. mental

7. confidence

8. skills

9. interaction

10. team

11. trophies

12. league

E 1. loser   2. isolate

3. straighten   4. active

5. success   6. catch

7. mend   8. hinder

Words within Words (p. 22)

A **Accessories** - suggestions:

score, scare, cases, raise, rises, roses, arise, erase, soars, cress, scar, sees, rice

B **Participation** - suggestions:

train, acorn, tonic, panic, tiara, apron, attic, paint, tonic, trip, cart, pain, pint

Painting and Drawing (p. 22-23)

A **blue** – azure, navy, turquoise, teal
red – ruby, crimson, scarlet, cherry
green – sage, olive, lime, emerald
yellow – amber, gold, lemon, sand

B 1. decorate   2. reproduce

3. picture   4. painter

5. combine   6. draw

7. colour   8. carving

C 1. MOSAIC
2. ORIGAMI
3. TEXTILE
4. PALETTE
5. CHALK
6. TESSELLATION
7. GALLERY
8. COLLAGE

D 1. paintbrush
2. outline
3. watercolour
4. brushstroke
5. overlap

E 1. face and figure
(others are pictures)
2. technique and line
(others are colour)
3. cup and kiln
(others are pottery)
4. special and similarity
(others are difference)
5. bush and tree
(others are scenery)
6. background and perspective
(others are brush strokes)

F 1. red 2. orange
3. yellow 4. green
5. blue 6. indigo
7. violet

Power and Conquest (p. 24-25)

A 1. creation 2. proof
3. culture 4. object
5. order 6. old
7. reference 8. period

B 1. warrior 2. runes
3. plunder 4. Norse
5. hoard 6. navigate
7. seafaring 8. fjord

C 1. inventor 2. explorer

3. ruler 4. dictator
5. settler 6. invader
7. survivor 8. conqueror
Challenge: traitor

D 1. MEN 2. ATE
3. RID 4. OR
5. AT 6. AN

E zoology – animals
astrology – star signs
psychology – mind
ecology – environment
sociology – society
ornithology – birds

F **working class** – servant, serf, labourer,
domestic, peasant, farmhand
nobility – sir, duchess, lady, earl,
baron, aristocrat, duke, lord
rulers – dictator, monarch, emperor,
king, president, queen

Writers and Forms of Writing (p. 26-27)

A 1. author 2. poet
3. novelist
4. playwright or dramatist
5. biographer
6. journalist or reporter

B 1. COVER
2. TITLE
3. CONTENTS
4. GLOSSARY
5. BLURB
6. SPINE

C footnote, format, crossword,
backstage, deadline, newspaper,
keypad, brainstorm
Extension: bookmark, bookshelf,
bookseller, bookbinder, bookable,
bookend, bookkeeper, bookmaker,
bookworm

D 1. tale, dramatist
2. poem, article

3. film, play
4. book, radio
5. criminal, villain
6. tell, convince

E 1. gothic   2. fable
3. spy   4. western
5. myth   6. sci-fi
7. crime   8. fantasy

F 1. air   2. gold
3. good   4. heart
5. monster   6. heart
7. twinkle   8. inch

Words within Words (p. 28)

A Archaeology - suggestions:

large, royal, clear, chore, layer, glare, glory, grace, grey, real, core, acre, cage,

B Literature - suggestions:

title, treat, trail, alter, ruler, eater, tear, teal, real, reel, tree, liar, late, rare

Transport (p. 30-31)

A air – space shuttle, balloon, glider, airship, helicopter
land – coach, moped, tram, scooter, truck
water – yacht, ferry, dinghy, hovercraft, liner, gondola

B 1. VAN   2. GLIDER
3. YACHT   4. TRAIN
5. CARAVAN   6. BICYCLE

C 1. HULL   2. STERN
3. ANCHOR   4. MAST
5. PORTHOLE   6. TILLER

D 1. quicken   2. capacity
3. length   4. speed
5. fast   6. vehicle
7. slow   8. climb

E 1. taxicab

2. windshield
3. lifeboat
4. hovercraft
5. seatbelt
6. carpark
7. motorway and highway
8. passport and airport

F 1. foot
2. horses (or camels)
3. camels (or horses)
4. wheel
5. transportation
6. century
7. steam
8. goods
9. leisure
10. aeroplane

The Environment (p. 32-33)

A 1. recycle, protect
2. typhoon, flood
3. save, gases
4. wildlife, forest
5. weather, world
6. die, cool

B ecosystem, oil slick, rainforest, renewable energy, ozone layer, global warming

C 1. rest and reward
(others mean recycle)
2. pollute and solar
(others mean effect)
3. jaguar and parrot
(others are primates)
4. violet and sand
(others are green)
5. purify and clean
(others mean ruin)
6. package and plastic
(others mean rubbish)

D recover, renew, reclaim, decompose, de/reforestation, refresh, decrease, replant, degrade, defrost, restore, recycle

E 1. lean (renewable and)
2. team (climate ambassador)
3. once (pollution ceases)
4. stop (rainforest operates)
5. test (drought estimate)
6. also (global solar)

F **energy** – 'work or activity'
global – 'all the world'
ecology–'study of where you live'
solar – 'from the sun'
conservation – 'keeping the same'
fertile – 'productive or fruitful'

Earth and Sky (p. 34-35)

A Mercury, Venus, Earth, Mars, Jupiter, Saturn, Uranus and Neptune

B 1. PIT   2. LIP
3. COP   4. HER
5. MEN   6. LIT
7. TAT   8. NET

C supernova, spacecraft, stardust, wavelength, moonbeam, sundial

D 1. constellation 2. rocket
3. observatory 4. gravity
5. eclipse   6. orbit
7. meteorite 8. satellite

E 1. path   2. air
3. turn   4. cover
5. stage   6. moon
7. galaxy   8. strange

F 1. Newton   2. gravity
3. force   4. ground
5. football 6. Earth
7. sun   8. planets
9. weightless 10. space

Words within Words (p. 36)

A **Environment** - suggestions:

event, timer, movie, metre, never, merit, nerve, enter, minor, miner, vein, vent

B **Transportation** - suggestions:

train, sport, onion, pasta, stain, patio, satin, start, apron, apart, ports, oats

Area and Shape (p. 38-39)

A 1. pentagon   2. hexagon
3. heptagon   4. octagon
5. nonagon   6. decagon

B 1. half   2. hundred
3. not   4. one
5. thousand   6. three

C 1. angle   2. side
3. area   4. diameter
5. volume   6. vertex
7. perimeter   8. circumference

D 1. KITE   2. CIRCLE
3. CUBE   4. SPHERE
5. TRIANGLE 6. PYRAMID
7. SQUARE   8. OCTAGON

E **2D** – circle, parallelogram, rectangle, triangle
3D – pyramid, cone, sphere, cube
shape measurement – area, diameter, volume, angle

F 1. MET   2. TAG
3. RAM   4. MEN
5. TAN   6. APE

Numbers (p. 40-41)

A 1. plus   2. minus
3. same   4. times
5. approximate 6. share
7. leftover   8. part

B 1. prime   2. denominator
3. integer   4. ratio
5. numerator   6. factor
7. fraction   8. multiple

C 1. TEAM (approximate amount)
2. DOME (do mental)
3. TEND (often division) SEAS (is easier)
4. OWED (now educated)

D 1. subtract, divide

2. right, approximate
3. months, weeks
4. whole, 100%
5. four sixths, a half
6. 81, 49

E 1. 365   2. 12
3. 28   4. 29
5. 52   6. 7
7. 24   8. 60

F 1. far – farther / further and farthest / furthest
2. great – greater and greatest
3. easy – easier and easiest
4. difficult – more difficult and most difficult
5. expensive – more expensive and most expensive
6. little – less and least

Statistics (p. 42-43)

A 1. table   2. pictogram
3. bar graph   4. pie chart
5. line graph   6. venn diagram

B 1. RAG   2. FOR
3. CAT   4. RAM
5. AIR   6. PAR

C 1. **BAR** – a block, to prevent something or someone
2. **PLOT** – to mark points on a chart, to plan something, patch of land
3. **FORM** – a document, to shape something

D 1. The median is the middle score. (last)
2. We can calculate mode by ordering data. (graph)
3. A sample is a section of the population. (choose)

E 1. sherbet lemons and chocolate
2. cola cubes
3. Ali

4. Joni and Benjy
5. Benjy and Ali

F 1. DATA
2. AVERAGE
3. PICTOGRAM
4. TABLE
5. MEDIAN

Words within Words (p. 44)

A **Parallelogram** - suggestions:

grape, opera, polar, pearl, glare, molar, aroma, legal, ample, leap, rage, more

B **Questionnaire** - suggestions:

quite, quiet, stair, stare, snort, quits, noise, raise, outer, eaten, nurse, rose

Word Classes (p. 46)

A 1. happily
2. slowly
3. painfully
4. sadly
5. terribly
6. hopefully
7. fast (no change)
8. joyfully

B with and without, above and beneath, after and before, towards and away, including and excluding, inside and outside.

C 1. when   2. who
3. whose   4. which
5. where   6. whom
7. which   8. whose
9. when   10. whom

Prefixes (p. 47)

A 1. un-   2. mis-
3. ir-   4. im-
5. non-   6. ir-
7. in-   8. mis-

9. im-   10. non-
11. un-   12. mis-

B **pre-** means before
re- means again
post- means after
fore- means in front of
ex- means former

C 1. **pre-** making pre-school, prearrange, premature
2. **fore-** making foreground, forehead, foresight
3. **ex-** making ex-girlfriend, ex-army, export
4. **post-** making post-date, post-war, post-mortem
5. **re-** making replay, replace, rewrite

D 1. **nona-** meaning 9
2. **centi-** meaning 100
3. **deca-** meaning 10
4. **kilo-** meaning 1000
5. **hept-** meaning 7
6. **pent-** meaning 5

Homographs (p. 48)

A 1. watch   2. bank
3. minute   4. chest
5. bat   6. tear
7. present   8. can

B 1. **bear** – mammal; to put up with or tolerate
2. **saw** – tool for cutting; past tense of 'to see'
3. **wind** – weather; to turn around; to be 'winded'
4. **fair** – festival or fete; pleasant or reasonable; light colour
5. **well** – store for water below ground; fine or good
6. **wave** – water at the sea; hand gesture

C 1. 'boat' is not a homograph

2. 'snow' is not a homograph
3. 'ribbon' is not a homograph
4. 'sea' is not a homograph
5. 'wrong' is not a homograph
6. 'fun' is not a homograph
7. 'hour' is not a homograph
8. 'tree' is not a homograph

Synonyms (p. 49)

A 1. nervous   2. thrilled
3. uncertain   4. resentful
5. motivated   6. optimistic

B danger – hazard
simple – easy
coronet – crown
profession – occupation
dwell – live
lift – elevate

C 1. devious   2. daring
3. infantile   4. dormant
5. change   6. detain
7. inhale   8. vessel

D LOOK – observe, watch, glance, stare, etc.
SCARY – frightening, petrifying, horrific, etc.
FAST – quick, speedy, pacy, etc.

Antonyms (p. 50)

A ancient and modern, foe and ally, fake and genuine, reckless and cautious, plain and elaborate, innocent and guilty

B 1. cultivated   2. vacant
3. deliberate   4. amateur
5. methodical   6. shallow
7. modest   8. miserable

C 1. C essential   2. C inactive
3. D private   4. A tidy
5. D accomplish
6. B release

Word Combinations (p. 51)

A
1. in
2. for
3. by
4. at
5. on

B
go- to sleep, online, astray
take – a look, turns, responsibility
make – a difference, the bed, a decision
pay – a visit, a compliment, attention

C
1. densely
2. pleasantly
3. closely
4. tightly
5. dimly
6. highly

Grammar Definitions (p. 52)

adjective - a 'describing' word which describes a noun

adverb – a word which gives you more information about a verb, often 'how' something is done. Many end in '-ly'.

pronoun – a word which replaces a noun

prefix – added to the start of a word to change the meaning

suffix – added to the end of a word, typically verb endings or used to change the word class

homograph – word which is spelt the way but has different meanings or words from different word classes

synonym – a word with a similar meaning

antonym – a word with the opposite meaning

collocation – a known combination of 2 words, often from different word classes

Similes and Metaphors (p. 54)

A
1. S
2. M
3. M
4. S
5. M
6. S

B kangaroo court, wolf down your food, bull by the horns, duck out, ants in your pants, monkey around

C
1. as busy as a bee
2. as quiet as a mouse
3. as slippery as an eel
4. as wise as an owl
5. as slow as a snail
6. as strong as an ox
7. as free as a bird
8. as sick as a dog

Personification (p. 55)

A
1. groaned
2. stroked
3. winked
4. refused
5. danced
6. controlled

B
1. heart
2. limb
3. mind
4. coat
5. eyes
6. mouth

C
1. comforting
2. determined
3. lazy
4. thoughtful
5. spiteful
6. stubborn

Sound Words (p. 56)

A
1. alliteration
2. assonance
3. alliteration
4. sibilance
5. alliteration or assonance
6. sibilance

B Any options are fine, as long as they start with the same letter as the number and are adjectives and verbs, with the latter in the past tense.

C
1. lonely
2. broken
3. many
4. scorching
5. refreshing
6. green
7. aching
8. delicious

Onomatopoeia (p. 57)

A
1. sputter
2. murmuring
3. blurted
4. whisper
5. retching
6. squirted
7. blared
8. crunched

B cat and purr, owl and hoot, bacon and sizzle, lion and roar, tap and drip, glass and smash, balloon and pop, bee and hum, rocket and zoom

C 1. howling   2. grating
3. babble   4. crunch
5. thud   6. gasping

Genre   (p. 58)

A **fantasy** – quest, elves, creature, sword, king
ghost – midnight, spirit, graveyard, haunted house
sci-fi – inter-planetary, deep space, AI, clone, galactic, alien
war – bombsite, front line, evacuee, military, bunker

B knowledge and ignorance,
love and hate, good and evil,
forgiveness and revenge,
hero and villain, bravery and cowardice,
dark and light,
poverty and wealth

C 1. biography   2. haiku
3. parable   4. ballad
5. novella   6. dystopian

Writing about Fiction   (p. 59)

A 1. shaded and gloomy
2. jubilant and upbeat
3. melancholy and depressing
4. light-hearted and comical
5. haunting and fearful

B 1. meditated   2. studied
3. investigated   4. reflected
5. considered   6. examined

C **sight** – any object is acceptable
smell – burning smell, whiff of decay
touch – prickly, stinging, damp, half-choking, spiky
sound – breathing heavily, low hum, tinny radio sound

Vocabulary for Literature Definitions   (p. 60)

simile – a comparison of 2 things, using 'as' or 'like'
metaphor – a comparison of 2 things which suggests that one thing 'is' another, which is not literally true
idiom – well-known saying which comes from
a particular language or culture
personification – referring to an animal or thing as if it was human
alliteration – repeating the same sound at the beginning of words
sibilance – repetition of 's' sound
assonance – repetition of vowel sound
onomatopoeia – word which sounds like its meaning
genre – type of fiction or story
antithesis - opposite

Comprehension   (p. 62)

A 1. hugely   2. real
3. work   4. inner
5. order   6. cunning
7. considering   8. continuously

B 1. talent   2. annoyed
3. rivals   4. staring
5. important   6. division
7. calm   8. disturbing

Root Words   (p. 63)

A 1. form   2. act
3. manage   4. honest
5. hope   6. luck
7. heat   8. connect

B The prefix must go in the front and suffix at the end. The resulting word must use the root word and be spelt correctly. The following are possible answers.

	root word	with a prefix	with a suffix
1.	happy	unhappy	happiness, happier
2.	plant	replant	planting, plantation
3.	correct	incorrect	correction, corrected
4.	place	replace, misplace	placed, placement
5.	do	redo, undo	doing, don't
6.	like	dislike, unlike	liked, likeable
7.	clear	unclear	clearance, clearing
8.	view	review, preview	viewing, viewed

C multi – many, astro – star, bio – life, micro – small, ethno – race, therm – heat, cosmo – world, meter – measure

Cloze (p. 64)

A 1. education 2. primary
3. secondary 4. knowledge
5. subjects 6. qualities
7. socialising 8. activities

B 1. thought 2. code
3. setting 4. levels
5. motivated 6. feedback
7. score 8. screen
9. online 10. challenge

C 1. ball – the rest are connected to badminton
2. camera – the others are about drama
3. rubber – you can write or draw with the others
4. cod – the rest are shellfish

Word Relationships (p. 65)

A **male** – uncle, grandfather, nephew, son
female – mother, wife, niece, nanny
not stated – in-law, fiancé, grandchild, cousin

B professor, teacher, doctor, musician, photographer, librarian, actor, veterinarian

C fin – fish, rind – lemon, chapter – book, leg – table, sole – shoe, spring – seasons
1. plant 2. hand
3. car 4. chair or sofa
5. bread 6. castle

Shuffle (p. 66)

A 1. Pirates wear eyepatches and hunt treasure. **Extra word**: ship.
2. Dracula has huge teeth and wears a black cloak. **Extra word**: blood.
3. The wolf plotted to eat the three little pigs. **Extra word**: house.
4. The Minotaur lived deep in a labyrinth. **Extra word**: mountain.
5. Lord Voldemort talked to snakes and was a dangerous magician. **Extra word**: wand.
6. Trunchbull loved to throw little children. **Extra word**: school.

B 1. violet 2. bronze
3. ebony 4. hazel
5. salmon 6. burgundy
7. teal 8. ivory

Degrees of Meaning (p. 67)

A The answers must be spelt correctly.
1. strange, stranger, strangest
2. beautiful, more beautiful, most beautiful

3. many, more, most
4. thin, thinner, thinnest
5. rare, rarer, rarest
6. scary, scarier, scariest
7. handsome, more handsome, most handsome
8. big, bigger, biggest.

B
1. gigantic
2. baking
3. exhausted
4. disfigured
5. enraged
6. bewildered
7. repulsed
8. remorseful

Vocabulary, Meaning and Context Tasks (p. 68)

A thoughtful, mischievous, baffled, crestfallen, ashamed, enraged

B Order is: d, a, c, f, b, e
a = 2, b = 5, c = 3, d = 1, e = 6, f = 4

C
1. bothered
2. tormented
3. disturbed
4. unsettled

Levels of Formality (p. 70)

A
1. cousin
2. grandmother
3. brother
4. child
5. sister
6. mother

B
1. hello
2. How are you?
3. goodbye
4. my apologies
5. thank you
6. fantastic

C
1. they have
2. we had OR we would
3. I will
4. will not
5. can not
6. you will

D
1. mate
2. as soon as possible
3. road
4. number
5. by the way
6. laugh out loud
7. people
8. got to go

Speech (p. 71)

A **angry** – barked, hissed, screeched
surprised – gaped, gasped, exclaimed
sad – bawled, cried, moaned
upbeat – joked, chuckled, jested

B as nutty as a fruitcake, as old as time, sleeps like a baby, babe in the woods, like a kid in a sweet shop, jack of all trades, a real pain in the neck

C
1. bragged
2. proclaimed
3. reassured
4. whined
5. reprimanded
6. refused
7. evaluated
8. queried

Linking Ideas (p. 72)

A **adding** – also, additionally, too
ordering – firstly, lastly, secondly
difference – but, however, unlike this

B tomorrow – the day after, now – at present, yesterday – the day before, sooner – earlier, meanwhile – at the same time, next – following

C
1. whenever
2. because
3. if
4. so
5. until

Creating Characters (p. 73)

A
1. logical
2. outspoken
3. absent-minded
4. eccentric
5. self-centred
6. astute
7. considerate
8. devoted

B chiselled cheekbones, oval face, tangled hair, hazel eyes, clumsy gait, upturned nose

C
1. rosy
2. unruly
3. full
4. sleek
5. obese
6. stubby
7. withdrawn
8. sullen

Settings with Attitude (p. 74)

A
1. cobweb
2. meadow
3. empty
4. derelict
5. glacial
6. bunting

B **positive** – liberating, calm, pleasant, familiar, warm, ideal
negative – damp, dank, jagged, miserable, faint
neutral – green, main, short, near

C **war** – shell, armoury, troop
sport – pitch, champion, award
western – horse, saloon, arrow
biography – date, family, achievement
historical – aristocrat, past, manor
fantasy – charm, villain, treasure

Attitude and Tone (p. 75)

A joyous – heartbroken, relaxed – tense, forgiving – vengeful, humorous – serious, dream-like – nightmarish, purposeful – directionless

B
1. passionate 2. fearful
3. comforting 4. depressed
5. sarcastic 6. furious

C
1. upset 2. thrilled
3. arrogant 4. optimistic
5. loving 6. thoughtful
7. zany 8. bold

Creative Vocabulary Definitions (p. 76)

contraction – shortened version of words, using apostrophe to show missing letters
formal language – correct, polite form of language, used for most writing
informal language – casual or slang language, used for speech, poetry and creative forms
abbreviation – shortened version of a word, to save time, make it brief or use as jargon / slang
cohesion – structure and structural devices within a paragraph
coherence – structure and structural devices linking paragraphs and sections
tone – attitude of a writer towards a topic or the reader
mood – atmosphere created, often in a story

or creative piece of writing, linked to genre

Adding and Taking Letters (p. 78)

A Any answer is acceptable if it makes a real word and the order of the letters is not changed. Some possibilities are listed.
1. Add 'l' to make 'blend' or 's' to make 'bends'.
2. Add 't' to make 'store' or 'h' to make 'shore' or 'p' to make 'spore' or 'n' to make 'snore'.
3. Add 't' to make 'stand'.
4. Add 's' to make 'steam' or 'teams'.
5. Add 'd' to make 'dared' or 's' to make 'dares'.
6. Add 'b' to make 'broad' or 's' to make 'roads'.
7. Add 'r' to make 'break' or 's' to make 'beaks'.
8. Add 'r' to make 'sport'.

B
1. RACE or RAGE or RAKE or RATE or RAVE or RAZE.
2. HEAP or HEMP
3. SHOW or SLOW or STOW.
4. VARY.
5. DRAB.
6. VAST.
7. SOLE or SOLO.
8. BATE or BATH.

C
1. move 'o' to make **fund** and **hoard**
2. move 'h' to make **torn** and **hearth**
3. move 'b' to make **tale** and **bless**
4. move 'r' to make **chat** and **insert**
5. move 'c' to make **lamp** and **cable** or 'm' to make 'clap' and 'amble'
6. move 'f' to make **sits** and **rifle**

Hidden Words (p. 79)

A
1. eat, ate 2. rib
3. tin 4. vat, tor
5. van, ant 6. pen, den
7. rid 8. and

B
1. data
2. dart
3. many
4. tear
5. urge
6. prow
7. idea
8. best

C
1. SHOE – hose and hoes
2. TIRE – tier and rite
3. EATS – east, seat, sate, teas
4. SNOW – sown and owns
5. NOSE – ones and eons
6. FOWL – wolf and flow
7. BRAG – garb and grab
8. PETS – pest and step

Relationships (p. 80)

A
1. **ingredients** – broccoli, vinegar, basil, garlic, pepper, flour
2. **utensils** – rolling pin, tongs, spoon, grater, sieve, spatula
3. **recipes** – pasty, paella, trifle, stew

B
surgeon – scalpel, mechanic – spanner, seamstress – needle, chef – saucepan, barrister – wig,
police officer – truncheon,
gardener – rake, lifeguard – buoy

C
1. parsnip (others are fruit)
2. lunch (others happen in the afternoon or evening)
3. save (rest are 'buy' synonyms)
4. scooter (others are baby equipment)
5. bungalow (rest are part of a house)
6. cougar (different root word)

Missing in Action (p. 81)

A
1. country
2. patriotic
3. values
4. sky
5. shapes
6. colour
7. century
8. cross

B
1. RAG to make AVERAGE
2. WAR to make AWKWARD
3. PAN to make COMPANION
4. RAN to make TRANQUIL
5. TUB to make STUBBORN
6. ONE to make LONELINESS
7. RIP to make DESCRIPTION
8. BIN to make COMBINATION

C These must be spelt correctly.
1. UNKNOWN
2. CONCLUSION
3. AMATEUR
4. IGNORANT
5. INNOCENT
6. SUPPLY
7. FORBID
8. SEPARATE

Combining Words (p. 82)

A These can appear in any order, to a total of 8. Each word can only be used once.
ponytail, eggshell, snowdrift, standby, sweetheart, takeoff, stopwatch, stagecoach

B
1. 't' will make crest and trace
2. 'e' will make bruise and elect
3. 'y' will make hasty and yield
4. 'l' will make peril and latter
5. 't' will make deceit and tyrant
6. 'h' will make oath and humble
7. 't' will make inhabit and torment
8. 'd' will make weird and despise

C
1. lucky becomes *luckily*
2. kind becomes *kindly*
3. angry becomes *angrily*
4. basic becomes *basically*
5. magic becomes *magically*
6. tidy becomes *tidily*
7. scientific becomes *scientifically*
8. faithful becomes *faithfully*

Playing with Words (p. 83)

A Any route is possible as long as only 1 letter is changed at a time and there is no change in the order of letters.
1. STOP to FLEW
   A possible route is: STOP, SLOP, SLOW, SLEW, FLEW
2. FAST TO ROAD
   A possible route is: FAST, MAST, MOST, MOAT, GOAT, GOAD, ROAD
3. GOLD to DUST
   A possible route is: GOLD, FOLD,

FOOD, FOOT, LOOT, LOST, LUST, DUST

B Any words which can be made out of the letters is acceptable. Only use the letters which appear and do not double up if there is only one letter. Each letter can be used multiple times. With a 5-minute timer, 15 is a good score, 25+ very good and 30+ is excellent.

C
1. last word: **hungry** happy, hug, huge, hungry
2. last word: **approach** anger, angry, apple, approach
3. last word: **rash** rabbit, rail, rare, rash
4. last word: **nest** meal, mice, mope, nest
5. last word: **quick** quail, quaint, queen, quick
6. last word: **found** feign, fond, forest, found